The Poem as Green Girdle

University of Florida Monographs
Humanities Number 55

The Poem as Green Girdle:

Commercium in

Sir Gawain and the Green Knight

R. A. Shoaf

A University of Florida Book

University Presses of Florida
Gainesville

Library of Congress Cataloging-in-Publication Data

Shoaf, R. A. (Richard Allen), 1948–
  The poem as green girdle.

  (University of Florida monographs. Humanities; no. 55)
  "A University of Florida book."
  Bibliography: p.
  Includes index.
  1. Gawain and the Grene Knight.   2. Gawain—Romances—
History and criticism.   3. Commerce in literature.
4. Chivalry in literature.   5. Circumcision in literature.
I. Title.   II. Series
PR2065.G31S53   1984   821'.1   84–2285
ISBN 0–8130–0766–6

Printed in the United States of America
on acid-free paper

Contents

To

Robert E. Kaske

AVALON FOUNDATION PROFESSOR IN THE HUMANITIES
IN CORNELL UNIVERSITY

with respect and gratitude

Preface

In this essay, I combine two critical approaches for a reading of *Sir Gawain and the Green Knight.* The two are equally important. The first method is historical and unashamedly so. It assumes that poems have contexts—economic, legal, political, theological, to name a few—and that without an understanding of these contexts, appreciation of a given poem is diminished. Expressed negatively, this is the assumption that poems ought not to be isolated and impoverished in Procrustean beds of self-referentiality. Poems always mean more and other than themselves. And *Sir Gawain*, no exception, can fairly be said to be "about" the conflict in late fourteenth-century England, deep and of far-reaching significance, between chivalry and commerce as two systems of value.

At the same time, however, poems do also mean themselves. They are "about" their own processes, since without such self-consciousness they could not come to be. Any shaping of language—alliteration, for example—which looks to language for what is peculiar in language must be aware of its process. This datum is fundamental to the second method used here. That method might be called "poststructuralist," but that would be a misnomer. And, anyway, labels are unimportant. It is the method that matters, and I am not against method. On the contrary, I am for methods that are conscious of themselves as methods. Unconscious, complacent methodology is the bane of literary criticism.

The second method further assumes that a poem will also question its process. As a result, it will discover its iconicity—its formality and inherent closure. The discovery will interrupt that closure and prevent the poem's immunity from the world and life. The poem will seek life there where form or iconicity or indeed method threatens to rigorize language into stasis and indifference. The poem is alive itself and knows itself. The poem issued from a living mind. My second method is a questioning of that mind.

The two methods combined are a questioning of mind in its historical context. Nothing new about that—for which I am thankful. And yet, if I am right, the poem will be new—of which I am hopeful.

Sir Gawain and the Green Knight is a very old poem from the end of the fourteenth century. It was written, we are fairly certain, in the Northwest Midlands of England; who wrote it we do not know. It survives in only one manuscript, Cotton Nero A X of the British Library, as one of four remarkable poems in that manuscript all assumed to be by the same author. Whoever he was, he is one of the leading figures in the so-called Alliterative Revival of the fourteenth century in England. *Sir Gawain* has been edited many times, translated many times, commented upon many times. The present commentary will not be the last, by any means. I do hope, however, that it does last.

* * *

Several people contributed to the successful completion of this book. John Alford, Judson Allen, Stephen Barney, John Burrow, William Courtenay, Lars Engle, Helen Link, Maureen Quilligan, and Robert B. Shaw all gave advice, criticism, and encouragement at various times. I am fortunate to have such colleagues; I hope that I do not disappoint them sorely.

I would also like to recognize and thank the A. Whitney Griswold Research Fund in Yale College for the award of a grant to defray the costs of typing and copying the manuscript.

Finally, I would like to thank, too, the Graduate School of the University of Florida for making the publication of the manuscript possible.

Apparatus

Expecting my audience to include not only seasoned medievalists, already familiar with the traditional annotations for the works being discussed, but also a disparate group ranging from advanced scholars of literary theory to interested but uninitiated university students, I provide here some notes on abbreviations, texts, and translations. I trust this information will be helpful to some and not too intrusive for others.

Abbreviations

AfWb	*Tobler-Lommatzsch Altfranzösisches Wörterbuch*
AS	Anglo-Saxon
CCCM	*Corpus Christianorum Continuatio Medieualis*
CCSL	*Corpus Christianorum Series Latina*
CSEL	*Corpus Scriptorum Ecclesiasticorum Latinorum*
DACL	*Dictionnaire de archéologie chrétienne et de liturgie*
DL-FAC	*Dictionnaire Latin-Français des auteurs chrétiens*
EETS	The Early English Text Society
MED	*Middle English Dictionary*
OED	*Oxford English Dictionary*
PL	*Patrologia Latina* (ed. Migne)
PPl	*Piers the Plowman*
SGGK	*Sir Gawain and the Green Knight*
ST	*Summa Theologiae* of St. Thomas Aquinas
T-G-D	Tolkien-Gordon-Davis edition of *SGGK*

Conventional scholarly practice has been followed for abbreviations of standard works. A few examples follow.

For the *Summa Theologiae* of St. Thomas Aquinas, ST 3a. 69. 3 is a reference to the third part of the *Summa*, question number 69, article 3. MS Oxford Bodl. Hatton 71 refers to a manuscript in the Hatton collection, number 71, of the Bodleian Library in Oxford.

As for the works of medieval poets, "Chaucer, CT I A 2190," for example, refers to the *Canterbury Tales*, Fragment I (Group A), *The Knight's Tale*, line 2190; and PPl A. 10. 19 is a reference to *Piers the Plowman* by William Langland, the A-text, *passus* 10, line 19.

References to dictionaries take the following form: abbreviated title, letter of the relevant volume, column number; thus OED C: 1101, for example, refers to the volume for the letter C of the *Oxford English Dictionary*, column 1101. The same method applies to references to the *Middle English Dictionary*.

The usual abbreviations for the books of the Bible (for example, Matt., Deut.) appear throughout.

A Note on the Texts

The Latin text of the Bible consulted for this book was the thirteenth-century "Paris" version contained in J.-P. Migne, PL 28 and 29; the English translation cited throughout is the Douay-Rheims, which is available in many convenient editions.

The text of *SGGK* used throughout this book is that of J. R. R. Tolkien and E. V. Gordon, second edition by Norman Davis (Oxford: Oxford University Press, 1967; reprinted with corrections, Oxford: Oxford University Press, Clarendon Press, 1968), but I have routinely consulted also A. C. Cawley and J. J. Anderson, *Pearl, Cleanness, Patience, Sir Gawain and the Green Knight* (London: Dent, 1976).

Chaucer is cited from the second edition of *The Works* by F. N. Robinson (Cambridge: Houghton Mifflin, 1957); *Piers the Plowman* (PPl), from the edition by W. W. Skeat, 2 vols. (Oxford: Oxford University Press, 1886); Dante, *La Commedia secondo l'antica vulgata*, from the edition of the Società Dantesca Italiana by Giorgio Petrocchi, 4 vols. (Milan: Mondadori, 1966–67); and *Le Roman de la Rose*, from the edition by Felix Lécoy, 3 vols. (Paris: Champion, 1966–74).

A Note on Translations

Except as noted below, all translations in this book are my own. In my translations, I have sought clarity and usefulness before literal accuracy, on the one hand, or elegance, on the other. I have often had to be "freer" than perhaps is ideal, because the Latin I cite is liturgical or otherwise technical, but the greater ease of understanding thus made possible compensates, I hope, for any inaccuracy or inelegance.

For Dante's *Commedia*, I have used Charles Singleton's translation in the Bollingen Series, number 58 (Princeton: Princeton University Press, 1970–75). For *Le Roman de la Rose*, I have used the translation by Charles Dahlberg (Princeton: Princeton University Press, 1971).

The decision not to translate the text of *SGGK* was prompted mainly by misgivings about the distortion in argument that would have resulted: far too often an argument would have had to begin with comment on the translation before going on to any other issue. Numerous translations of *SGGK* are, of course, in print. For this book, I consulted, in verse, those by Marie Borroff, *Sir Gawain and the Green Knight: A New Verse Translation* (New York: Norton, 1967), and J. R. R. Tolkien, *Sir Gawain and the Green Knight, Pearl, and Sir Orfeo* (Boston: Houghton Mifflin, 1975), and, in prose, that of W. R. J. Barron, *Sir Gawain and the Green Knight* (New York: Barnes and Noble, 1974).

Introduction

How persistent Bertilak's Lady is. Late in the third fitt of *Sir Gawain*, as part of her effort to persuade Gawain to accept the green girdle, she asks him, "'Now forsake ȝe þis silke . . . / For hit is symple in hit-self?'" (lines 1846–47).[1] The question, we quickly catch on, is a lead-ing one. She continues with a description of the girdle that is signifi-cant for the poem's meaning:

> And so hit wel semez.
> Lo! so hit is littel, and lasse hit is *worþy;*
> Bot who-so knew þe *costes* þat knit ar þerinne,
> He wolde hit *prayse* at more *prys*, parauenture;
> For quat gome so is gorde with þis grene lace,
> While he hit hade hemely halched aboute,
> Þer is no haþel vnder heuen tohewe hym þat myȝt,
> For he myȝt not be slayn for slyȝt vpon erþe."
> (1847–54; emphasis added)

Four words in this description refer to the world of commerce: *worþy*, *costes*, *prayse*, and *prys*.[2] One of them, *costes*, is a pun: its basic meaning is something like 'quality', but on numerous occasions in the poem—and the present passage is a good example—its context suggests the homonym 'cost'. Two of these words, *prayse* and *prys*, are related as verb and corresponding noun. The noun *prys*, in addition to its com-mercial meaning, is rich in connotations from its pervasive role in me-dieval French *chansons de geste* and romances (AfWb 7: 1877–84). It occurs twelve times in *Sir Gawain*—the highest frequency of any word in the poem's commercial vocabulary. The last of the four words, *worþy*, enjoys many shades of meaning, but often its context insists on the meaning of 'value' in the commercial sense. In addition to these 4 words, 63 more of a similar type, comprising 2½ percent of the

1

poem's total vocabulary, occur almost 190 times (see Appendix). Small though it may be, this commercial vocabulary, as its role in the strategic description of the green girdle suggests, is an important part of the poem and its total effect.

* * *

A poem of comparisons and measurements, of doublings and tests, of games and covenants, *Sir Gawain* structures a vision of relativity and relationship in human exchange. I feel I must explain and justify these terms since they figure so prominently in the argument to follow. Their origin—and here origin means justification—is feudalism itself: feudalism is a phenomenon, in its largest as well as its smallest detail, of human relations. And *Sir Gawain* is indisputably a poem immersed in feudalism, hence also concerned with relationships. At the same time, *Sir Gawain* shows an equally obvious concern with commerce and economics. Relativity is, of course, a crucial element of both commerce and economics, for the concepts of weighing, measuring, testing, and evaluation are dominant in both; and all these depend on relativity—something is evaluated or measured relative to something else. Feudalism and commerce, then, motivate my frequent recourse in this argument to the notions of relativity and relationship.

The commercial vocabulary of *Sir Gawain* consistently informs its structure. Exchange–discourse, intercourse, currency (each a form of commerce)—accounts for a part of the poem's vocabulary and several of its central images and tropes ultimately because the poem is itself an economy in the sense that it is a dispensation or arrangement of media and mediation for the purpose of evaluating—better, 'assaying' (cf. 2362, 2457)—human civilization or, in the poem's word, *nurture* (919, 1661).[3]

Such evaluation or assaying begins as early as the very opening of the poem, where British civilization is shown to have a heritage of *tricherie* (4) descending from *superbum Ilium*.[4] The 'assaying' continues when Gawain, the *fyne fader of nurture* (919), betrays his host by concealing the latter's girdle only to be punished thereupon by an exposure to mortality so humiliating that he can never possibly forget it (2511–12). It culminates in Gawain's return to Arthur's court wearing the *syngne of surfet*, the *token of untrawþe* (2433, 2509, respectively), which, because the members of the court share it with him, signifies the court's meaning, too: Arthurian civilization is *worth* the green girdle. This is to say two things at once, that it is worth a great deal and that its worth has definite limits all the same.[5] Arthurian civilization and its ideal exemplar are not perfect and their imperfection is serious; but their awareness of their imperfection, expressed in their willingness to display the sign of that imperfection, grants them a freedom and a recourse from *superbia* which suggests that Britain may not repeat the Fall of Troy. Similarly, the poem itself, less a pentangle than a green girdle, less a fixed icon than a fluid sign, is aware of its own limits as art; and from that awareness it gains a beauty, a precision, and an importance that more ostentatious symbols must sacrifice.

In the study that follows, the ways in which the commercial vocabulary helps to locate the meaning of *Sir Gawain and the Green Knight* are demonstrated. First, it is argued that the old values of chivalry and feudalism were competing, unsuccessfully, with commercialism in the fourteenth century. Aware of the conflict between them, *Sir Gawain* attempts to reconcile these opposing forces through its vision of media and mediation in human affairs—its vision of man's middled and muddled estate that is somewhere between personal loyalties and abstract market forces. Motivating the reconciliation, the chapter goes on to suggest, are both Christian traditions and contemporary economic realities.

Next comes the suggestion that the specific Christian rite grounding the commercial vision of the poem is circumcision. Within the sacrament of penance, which is fundamental to the poem, the rite of circumcision functions as a source of imagery and of theological information. It is suggested by the *nirt* (2498) in the neck that Gawain receives from the Green Knight on New Year's Day, the day when the Church celebrates the Feast of the Circumcision. Authorizing the connection suggested here is the crucial fact that, liturgically, circumcision is understood to be a commerce between God and man—this, according to the antiphon "O admirabile commercium" sung during Laudes of the Feast of the Circumcision. This antiphon and subsequent commentaries on it illuminate the language and the setting of the exchange between Gawain and the Green Knight at the Green Chapel. Moreover, the sacramentality of circumcision, in light of late medieval sacramental theory, contributes to an understanding of that emphasis on signs and tokens that the poem introduces after Gawain's experiences at the Green Chapel (2398, 2433, 2509).

Chapters 3 and 4 contain an analysis of the numerous passages elsewhere in the poem in which the commercial vocabulary dominates. The exchange between Gawain and the Green Knight completes a process of commercialization (so I will call it) that began with Gawain's arrival at Hautdesert. That process involves the transformation of

Gawain, on the one hand, into a consumer and, on the other, into a merchant; Bertilak's Lady effects the one, Bertilak himself, the other. Having become consumer and merchant, Gawain can at last accept both his *prys* (2364) and, in the antiphon's formula, the inevitable consequence of that *prys*, or *nostram humanitatem*.

After an interlude for a summary of the entire argument up to that point, chapter 3 continues with an analysis of the seduction scenes. During these scenes, Bertilak's Lady traps Gawain into insisting on private values to the exclusion of his numerous relationships and their attendant duties. She convinces Gawain that everything has its price, and she effectively reduces him, in doing so, to a consumer. And when Gawain buys her word, as he finally does, it is because, as he himself says, he has become proud of her evaluation of him. The circumcision at the Green Chapel metaphorically cuts away this pride. Next, a survey of the covenant making between Bertilak, the Green Knight, and Gawain demonstrates the importance of law to the poem's commercial vision and situates the covenant making in a context of both medieval English contract law and Old Testament legalism. This section of the study concludes by demonstrating that Gawain becomes a "foxy" merchant in his dealings with Bertilak, so much so that he is able to overlook the breach of contract in his concealment of the green girdle. Like the fox which Bertilak hunts, Gawain pridefully works *with wylez* (1711). The circumcision metaphorically cuts away this pride, too.

The book culminates in an exploration of the connection between Gawain's *cowarddyse* and *couetyse* (2374) and the sin of idolatry. Texts contemporary with the poem, as well as earlier ones, affirm that covetousness and idolatry are sins inseparable from each other genetically; from this evidence arises the argument that the green girdle must replace the pentangle as Gawain's standard because, unlike the latter, it is so conventional and arbitrary a sign that it can never threaten to become an idol and thus a spur to covetousness. The poem's emphasis on signs and tokens, the argument maintains, is an integral part of its larger concern with order and meaning in civilization. Finally, it is suggested that the poem itself resembles the green girdle more than the pentangle. As a text, the poem insists on its conventionality and temporality in such a way as to affirm its concern with meaning and with the way in which meaning is made.

1

The Poem in Its Commercial Context

i. The Commercial Vision of
Sir Gawain and the Green Knight

Sir Gawain and the Green Knight's concern with mediation, relativity, relationships, and value is a response to one of the most pressing and
complicated social issues of its day. Commercialism and chivalry, two
value systems, were competing in a very uneven contest. Indeed, later
medieval English history is the chronicle of the triumph of the one,
commercialism, over the other.[1] If *Sir Gawain*'s vision of the possible
reconciliation between the two systems is difficult to appreciate at this
remove in time, it may well have been just as difficult for contempo-
raries of the poem. They would have had to see, as we must, that the
power of money to displace and to represent (by substitution)—so
many soldiers, for example, or so many acres of a once intact estate—
depends on relativity and opposition, just as the power of language to
signify chivalric or any other values depends on relativity and opposition. They would have had to see, as must we, *Sir Gawain*'s vision of
mediation in human affairs—its vision of man's middled and muddled estate.

This vision depends on the commercial vocabulary and, most heav-
ily perhaps, on two words in particular, *prys* and *costes*. After the
Green Knight has tested Gawain and found him wanting (though
wanting less than any other man), he declares: "'As perle bi þe quite
pese is of *prys* more, / So is Gawayn, in god fayth, bi oþer gay knyʒtez'"
(2364–65; emphasis added). As important as the content of this conclusion is its form—the form of an analogy of proper proportionality
whose essential characteristic is similarity of relations.[2] Gawain is compared, he is measured, he is related to other items: the Green Knight
fixes the *prys* of Gawain even as he acknowledges the worth of Gawain; he establishes the *costes* of Gawain (see 2360). The standard,
within the analogy, by which Gawain is measured is the pearl. Gawain
is like a pearl, a pearl of great price. Once he has priced Gawain on
the market of chivalric values, the Green Knight goes on to absolve

the man who cannot of his kind, even though he is like a pearl, be absolute: "'I halde þe polysed of þat ply3t, and pured as clene / As þou hadez neuer forfeted syþen þou watz fyrst borne'" (2393–94). As his words suggest, he absolves Gawain of the guilt of pride (*surquidré*, 311, 2457)—pride, which is the disdain of relativity—since the newborn, who is as yet without a history, is accordingly not subject to relativity, or that fundamental human experience of measurement and comparison in which pride (or humility) is forged: all newborns, even those deformed and doomed to die, are simply good. Moreover, in restoring Gawain to the innocence of infancy, the Green Knight absolves him of all *forfeting* where *to forfet* means not 'to transgress' but 'to pay the fine or the penalty for transgression' (see chap. 2 at n. 14). The Green Knight absolves Gawain of a fine or debt: he redeems him from the debt of original sin (Burrow 1965:157; chap. 4 at n. 10).

Once absolved of the guilt of pride, Gawain must wear the sign of relativity and relationship—the *syngne of surfet* (2433), the *token of vntrawþe* (2509)—which, as a sign, is intrinsically relative to that which it is *not*, or, moderation and truth. Just as signification itself depends on the structure of difference and opposition—the phoneme *p* is similar to but different from the phoneme *b* with the result that 'pit' and 'bit' are intelligible lexemes within the English language (Saussure 1966: 111–22)—so, too, the green girdle, as sign, depends on the pentangle, Gawain's shield, which disappears from the poem after its lengthy introduction precisely because the green girdle, having been identified alongside of it, replaces it.[3] The point needs some emphasis. Readers of *Sir Gawain* often note the poem's insistent doublings. Hautdesert doubles Camelot; Bertilak's court doubles Arthur's; the later Christmas feast doubles the earlier one; and so on (Allen 1971:145–49). Similarly, the green girdle doubles the pentangle. If the pentangle is ostentatiously Gawain's standard at the beginning of the adventure, the girdle is just as ostentatiously his standard at the end. Moreover, Gawain (and the poem) concentrates on the girdle at the end to the exclusion of any further mention of the pentangle. This doubling, therefore, appears to go further than the numerous others. These others serve to define and to distinguish shades of meaning and of value: there is, for instance, a more pristine simplicity and a greater felicity about Bertilak's court in comparison with and as opposed to Arthur's court. The opposition between the pentangle and the girdle, however, not only defines and distinguishes their relative values; it also fundamentally alters Gawain's—which is to say, the Arthurian—world. The green girdle returns to Camelot with Gawain: it is, as it were, part of the other world brought back to this world. As such, it is the foundation of a *new* definition, one that transcends as it also incorporates the older definition represented by the pentangle. Once back at Camelot, Gawain may still bear the sign of perfection (the pentangle), although the poem is silent on this; but he wears the sign of imperfection *a bende abelef hym aboute* (2517), and it is the more visible sign. So visible, in fact, that it is probably truer to say that Gawain wears a *sign*—something relative, measured, and contingent—for the first time in full and chastened consciousness of the mysterious ubiquity of signs.

Henceforth, Gawain must live with relativity and relationships, the human experience of measurement and comparison, despite the constant temptation to succumb to pride. He must live with and know he lives with verbal, economic, and chivalric systems of *value* which, because they *are* systems of value, are intrinsically relative, comparative, and measured. As the *fyne fader of nurture* (919) Gawain mediates between nature and fortune, or, perhaps, one could say history. I think all readers of the poem would agree that at some level the Green Knight is a figure of nature; there is evidence, in addition, that Bertilak's Lady and Morgne la Faye figure the two faces of fortune.[4] Gawain experiences his trials and tests, then, at the hands of the two great ministers of this sublunary sphere; they evaluate in him and through him the *nurture* of Arthurian civilization. Gawain, the *fyne fader of nurture*, is the ideal embodiment of the values of Arthurian civilization; he is the measure, the standard for all knights and ladies who would participate in that civilization, live in its world, draw on its store of meaning. But he is himself measured and tested at Hautdesert and the Green Chapel. Between fortune, or history, and nature, Gawain experiences the radical contingency of human institutions—be they castles or chivalric manners—upon the limitations to human striving.[5] Chief among these limitations is the inevitable tumescence of pride. As the text has it:

> 'Weldez non so hyȝe hawtesse
> Þat ho [Morgne la Faye] ne con make ful tame—
>
> 'Ho wayned me vpon þis wyse to your wynne halle
> For to assay þe surquidré, ȝif hit soth were
> Þat rennes of þe grete renoun of þe Round Table.'
> (2454–58)

Gawain, we can say without fear of contradiction, is at least *tame* when he returns to Camelot; his pride has been chastened (see 2437–38).

And this because he has learned that he does not measure up. More. He has learned that he is subject to measuring (Davenport 1978:189–90). The measure is measured. This is the insight at the heart of the poem's insistence on doubling. Comparison or doubling is the elementary structure of value and meaning; and the poem is concerned with the way value and meaning are made, so much so, in fact, that Gawain's experience is the experience of meaning in a human world: he learns what it means to have a meaning.

The process is manifold. First, Bertilak's Lady introduces Gawain into relativity as she seduces him into becoming a consumer. Next, Bertilak himself transforms Gawain into a merchant, or perhaps it would be better to say that he draws out of Gawain the merchant latent in every man. Gawain is both consumer and native merchant in a kind of rhythm, a basic human rhythm of exchange, that his testers control. Finally, the Green Knight prices Gawain, who can at last appreciate that he does have a price and that he is relative and involved in relationships, not absolute. Note well that the humbling of Gawain's pride is thus consistent and simultaneous with the determination of just how valuable he really is: negation (of pride) produces a positive (Gawain's *prys*). We will see similar structuring of meaning again in the poem.

As a result of the testing of Gawain, which is the testing of the *nurture* of Arthurian civilization, authentic exchange replaces prideful insistence on static absolutes. When Gawain returns, the court members are willing to exchange meanings with him. Gawain has brought back with him a new understanding of *nurture*. Henceforth, *nurture* will not presume to possess the ideal. On the contrary, because it is subject to nature and fortune, *nurture* must acknowledge the transcendence of the ideal. Acknowledging this transcendence, *nurture* accepts that it can only incarnate the ideal—that is to say, mediate the ideal to the individual who aspires to it, always allowing for the slack in the individual's humanity. "'Þou art *not* Gawain'" (2270; emphasis added), cries the Green Knight after Arthur's finest knight flinches from the blow. The name *Gawain* represents an ideal, transcending nature and fortune, which no man can "possess," no matter how great his *nurture* (cf. Davenport 1978:190–91). He can only, on the contrary, through that *nurture* participate in the ideal, distorting it, however, even as he participates in it. To live with such a negative, which is also an opposition and a measurement, and thus to try to merit his name by means of the ideal that he is *not*, Gawain must sacrifice his pride and become a knight of the sign, the green girdle.[6]

ii. Commerce and Christianity

Informing the commercial vision of *Sir Gawain and the Green Knight* are two related but distinct phenomena. First is the role of commercial discourse in Christianity. Beginning with Scripture itself, *commercium* is a crucial concept, generating a nearly inexhaustible supply of imagery for the relationships between God and man. The theology of redemption suggests itself as one obvious source of such imagery (Lyonnet and Sabourin 1970:46–224). The verb *redimere* means 'to buy back', and the New Testament abounds in significant examples of the term and its implications. Hence, for example, Mark 10. 45: "For the Son of Man also is not come to be ministered unto; but to minister and to give his life a redemption for many." Or, again, I Corinthians 6. 20: "For you are bought with a great price"; then, too, I Peter 2. 9: "But you are a chosen generation, a kingly priesthood, a holy nation, a purchased people." Related to the latter verse and of great importance to the *Gawain*-poet's other major work, *Pearl* (see 892–94), is Apocalypse 14. 3: "And they sang as it were a new canticle, before the throne and before the four living creatures and the ancients; and no man could say the canticle, but those hundred forty-four thousand, who were purchased from the earth." This is only a small sample which centers on just one term. To both could be added such passages as Colossians 2. 2–3: "That their hearts may be comforted, being instructed in charity and unto all riches of fullness of understanding, unto the knowledge of the mystery of God the Father and of Christ Jesus: In whom are hid all the treasures of wisdom and knowledge." These tropes are more than just ways of speaking: they are insights into the humanity of exchange and the exchanges of humanity. Perhaps the best measure of the importance of exchange in Scripture is the very idea of covenant itself. A covenant is in fact a commercial contract (OED C:1101). And in the later Middle Ages, this idea, expressed usually by the term *pactum* (Courtenay 1971:96–102; Hamm 1977:407–10), assumes extraordinary importance for English poetry. It is at the core of Langland's insistence on *redde quod debes*, Gower's passion for the *comune profit* (Peck 1978:xxi), and Chaucer's fascination with marriage. Equally important in Scripture and for Middle English poetry is the concept of debt which is explicit, of course, in the Lord's Prayer (Matt. 6. 12) and in the Church's teaching following St. Paul on the marriage debt (I Cor. 7. 3).

The Fathers of the Church continue Scripture's practice as they draw from the world of commerce for their meditations on the exchanges between God and man. Augustine writes, for example, "egit enim in cruce grande commercium (Upon the cross, he has completed the great exchange)."[7] Or, less terse though no less compelling,

> Attendite omnes homines, utrum ad aliud sint in hoc saeculo, quam nasci, laborare et mori. Haec sunt mercimonia regionis nostrae, ista hic abundant. Ad tales merces *Mercator ille* descendit. Et quoniam omnis mercator dat et accipit; dat quod habet et accipit, quod non habet; quando aliquid comparat, dat pecuniam, et accipit quod emit; etiam Christus in ista mercatura dedit et accipit. Sed quid accepit? Quod hic abundat, nasci, laborare, et mori. Et quid dedit? Renasci, resurgere et in aeternum regnare. O bone Mercator, eme nos. Quid dicam, eme nos, cum gratias agere debeamus, quia emisti nos![8]

> Mark this question everyone: whether there is anything else in this world other than to be born, to labor, to die. These make up the merchandise of our world, these things abound here. For such pay did that Merchant descend. And since every merchant gives and receives—that is, gives what he has and receives what he does not have, as, for example, when he buys something, he gives money and receives in exchange what he buys—just so, Christ in this negotiation gives and receives. But what does he receive? What but the things that here abound—to be born, to labor, to die? What did He give? To be reborn, to arise, and to reign throughout eternity. O good Merchant, buy us. What am I saying, buy us? when we ought rather to give thanks, that you have bought us.

Or again, perhaps even more explicit:

> Dignatus est assumere formam servi, et in ea nos vestire se: qui non est dedignatus assumere nos in se, non est dedignatus transfigurare nos in se, et loqui verbis nostris, ut et nos loqueremur verbis ipsius. Haec enim mira *commutatio* facta est, et divina sunt peracta *commercia*, mutatio rerum celebrata in hoc mundo *a negotiatore caelesti*: venit accipere contumelias, dare honores, venit haurire dolorem, dare salutem, venit subire mortem, dare vitam.[9]

> He thought it worthy to assume the form of a servant, and in that form to clothe us himself—He who did not think it unwor-

thy to take us up into Himself, who did not think it unworthy to transfigure us in Himself, and to speak our very words, so that we might also speak His words. For this marvelous exchange was made, these divine transactions accomplished, this alteration of affairs in our world consummated, all by the heavenly Merchant: He came to receive reproaches, to give honors; he came to drink grief and sickness, to give health and salvation; he came to undergo death, to give life.

To these examples numerous others from Augustine's works could be added and from the works of other Fathers as well.[10] But of more use here, perhaps, is an example from the very end of the Middle Ages. Gabriel Biel, the fifteenth-century nominalist theologian, argues (Oberman 1967:59) that "cum itaque terreno cesari debetur sensualis denarius sua imagine signatus et nomine circumscriptus . . . quanto magis reddendum est quod debemus deo, animam scilicet nostram sua imagine signatam, sanguine mundatam, virtutibus donis et sacramentorum characteribus circumscriptam (Since, therefore, to the earthly Caesar the sensual coin is owed, being stamped with his image and circumscribed with his name . . . how much more must we pay what we owe to God, namely our soul, stamped with His image, cleansed by His blood, circumscribed with the virtues and powers of his gifts and the marks and characters of his sacraments)." Numerous examples from the intervening 1,000 years could be adduced,[11] but these will suffice to demonstrate that *Sir Gawain* is well within the Christian tradition when it figures the exchanges between God and man as an economy of mediation.

iii. The Commercial Situation of Fourteenth-Century England

The second phenomenon at work in *Sir Gawain*'s commercial vision is the unprecedented economic upheaval that England experienced in the fourteenth century.[12] A combination of famines (1315–1322), plagues (1349 and subsequent attacks), and climatic change abruptly halted that almost uninterrupted growth of the preceding centuries that Professor Lopez (1976:167) has suggested we call the commercial revolution of the Middle Ages. If halted now, however, that revolution nonetheless had initiated mutations in social institutions and structures which emerge starkly in the aftermath of the early fourteenth-century crises. The most significant mutation, which occurred only gradually, was, to cite Professor Lopez again (155), "the general replacement of payments and tributes in kind (that is, in goods and services) by payments and tributes in cash or credit." Moreover,

> if credit on the whole tended to impoverish and enslave the inhabitants of the country, cash had the opposite effect. It enabled both lords and peasants to shop for a greater variety of market goods and spurred them to increase their marketable production in order to procure more cash: further, it loosened all inherited personal attachments to a master, a community and a routine. . . . The agrarian ideal of security based on permanent mutual obligations was slowly bending towards the commercial quest for opportunity based on temporary contractual agreements.[13]

Furthermore, "pressed by necessity, and much more aware of economic realities and relative values than their predecessors [the lords of the thirteenth and fourteenth centuries] took advantage of the increase in productivity and the more thorough circulation of money in the countryside" (Duby 1976:258). Money had begun to dissolve the masonry of feudalism.

This dissolution was more apparent after the Black Plague than it had ever been before: "The initial result of the series of plagues in the second half of the fourteenth century was a dramatic increase in the per capita wealth of the survivors; money, gold and silver plate, and durable goods of all sorts remained to be divided among perhaps one-third fewer people than before the plague" (Miskimin 1969:87). This increase in wealth led to "the enhanced demand for luxury products, partially met by an upgrading of diet but more dramatically visible in changes of taste favoring the conspicuous consumption of expensive items of personal adornment" (Miskimin 1969:135). Fewer people with more wealth and the resultant desire for conspicuous consumption constitute only one, if the most ostentatious, example of money's gradual triumph, however. In addition, and just as depressing to the old spirit of personal loyalty, was, for example, the very cheap renting of land that the peasantry enjoyed when the lesser nobility, who were often small landlords, were forced to break up their holdings because of scarce labor and exorbitant wages (Duby 1976:306–11; Kershaw 1976:111 and 122). These lesser nobility—who, according to Thorlac Turville-Petre (1977:40–47), were the major patrons of the Alliterative Revival—were frequent casualties of the economic crisis because "each time a landlord was driven to rent out more land, he thereby further undermined his economic position by making rents lower, grain cheaper, and labor more expensive. . . . [Furthermore] each new disaster suffered by the landlords enhanced the bargaining position of the peasants, so that attempts to resuscitate obsolete feudal burdens were foredoomed to failure" (Miskimin 1969:44–45). Finally, "legislation promulgated in many countries and designed to reduce the 'excessive' demands of wage earners tended, in fact, to create a kind of black market for labor, in which, since the legal wage rate was below the economic wage rate, the landlord was compelled to violate the law if he hoped to prevent labor from seeking alternative employment" (Miskimin 1969:30). Before such pressures, feudalism and what might be called chivalric aspiration had to sink exhausted and obsolescent.

A further example from a different sphere—though intimately connected with money, namely credit—will also be instructive. Edward III fought his French wars largely on borrowed money. Wool had become more valuable as collateral than as cloth. Hence, for example, "from the parliament of February 1338 [Edward] received some kind of authorization for preemption of half the wool in the kingdom (estimated at 20,000 sacks) . . . and on the security of this new grant he arranged with the Bardi and the Peruzzi for substantial loans" (McKisack 1959:157). But these were the very Italian banking houses that, because of his later failure to honor his many debts, Edward broke, the Peruzzi in 1343 and the Bardi in 1346 (Miskimin 1969:151). Wars fought on loans subsequently defaulted on were only one sign of the power, positive and negative, of money and credit. When to this sign are added others such as dry exchange and *contra-cambium*—gimmicks that were used to disguise usury and thus avoid ecclesiastical censure (Bernard 1972:323–27 and de Roover 1967: 33)—it becomes possible, even in such a bare sketch as the present one, to appreciate how pervasive money had become in the mid-fourteenth century—and how blatant its abuses (Duby 1976:259).

In such an environment *Sir Gawain and the Green Knight* was written. It was an environment in which men were increasingly aware of the exclusive triumph of a money economy. Hence, for example, Chaucer's and Langland's concerns and anxieties about money: the Wife of Bath's "'Winne whoso may, for al is for to selle.'" (III D 414); Will's outburst against false coiners and counterfeiters (A. 10. 19); not to mention the figure elsewhere in *Piers the Plowman* of Lady Meed. Not only poets but also theologians and philosophers, such as Fishacre or d'Ailly (Courtenay 1971:94–119), and social theorists, such as Nicholàs Oresme in his *De Moneta* and in his translation of the pseudo-Aristotelian *Oeconomica*, reflect this triumph of what is ultimately symbolic displacement—so many nobles *for* so much sex (cf. *The Miller's*

Tale I A 3256), so many pennies *for* so much bread, so many pounds *for* the conquest of France.

Perhaps the most telling indication of the changes that money had wrought is a development in the theology and the iconography of the seven deadly sins, a development crucial to understanding *Sir Gawain and the Green Knight*. According to Lester K. Little (1978:36), in the wake of money's takeover of human affairs, avarice became as important as pride in considerations of the root and cause of sin and evil:

> Until the end of the tenth century, pride was unreservedly dominant as the most important vice; writers who dealt with avarice tended to reduce it to a subcategory of pride. But in the eleventh century, Peter Damian heralded a significant change when stating unequivocally: "Avarice is the root of all evil." . . . Over two decades later he characterized the leading problem in contemporary monastic life as the love of money. . . . Pride in the meantime did not surrender its place of preeminence but was henceforth constrained to share that place with avarice.

With Gawain's curse on his *couetyse*, or 'avarice' (2374), the poem adds its own to the numerous voices, prior to it and contemporary with it, that were crying out against this sin which money especially inspires.[14] Although its tone is not moralistic and although its concern is not one of social reform, *Sir Gawain and the Green Knight* is enough a part of its time and place to see in the growth of commerce and of a money economy the need for a warning against *couetyse*. The poem differs from other texts—venality satires, for example (Yunck 1963:1–13)— being greater than they are, in this particular: if it knows that a man, even the very best of men, will succumb to avarice, it also affirms that he can rise again—through confession, penitence, and, above all, humility.

2

The Commerce of Circumcision
and the Role of Mediation

i. New Year's Day and the Feast of the Circumcision

The religious and the economic exchanges mapped by the commercial vision of *Sir Gawain and the Green Knight* culminate in the pricing of Gawain by the Green Knight on New Year's Day, one year to the day from his beheading at Gawain's hands: "'As perle bi þe quite pese is of *prys* more, / So is Gawayn, in god fayth, bi oþer gay kny3tez'" (2364–65; emphasis added). The day and its customs are important to the commercial vision of the poem. In the first place, New Year's Day is the Octave of Christmas and the day of the Feast of the Circumcision of Jesus.[1] On this day, Gawain receives a *nirt* in the neck from the Green Knight. The *nirt* is a wound that displaces and resembles the wound of circumcision; it is not, let me insist right away, allegorically the same thing as circumcision—it only suggests circumcision. The fundamental and far-reaching importance of this implied circumcision is visible in and from the liturgy of the feast. Given the *Gawain*-poet's devotion to the Christian liturgy and given his audience's undoubted familiarity with the liturgical significance of New Year's Day, the *nirt* in the neck is a brilliant strategy for evoking the numerous associations of the Feast of the Circumcision.[2] And these associations help to explain the pricing of Gawain—help us to understand exactly why it should be commercial discourse that the poem deploys when Gawain bleeds at the Green Chapel. Moreover, the sacramentality of circumcision, as it is explained by medieval theologians early and late, exposes the strategy of the entire poem.

Penitence, to be sure, is the dominant sacrament of the poem (Burrow 1965:127–33). The Green Knight himself affirms as much:

'Þou art *confessed* so clene, beknowen of þy mysses,
And hatz þe *penaunce* apert of þe poynt of myn egge. . . .'
(2391–92; emphasis added)

15

However, penitence by no means excludes the more archaic rite of circumcision. Indeed, theologically speaking, circumcision is itself a kind of penitence for original sin. Hence, there is, so to speak, room for the associations of the rite to inform Gawain's experience at the Green Chapel. The New Testament sacrament and the Old Testament rite combine to bring about Gawain's necessary humiliation and rectification. And their combination for this purpose also helps to explain the poem's studied indirection and allusiveness about the circumcision: its strategy demands *both* New *and* Old Testament resonances at the moment of Gawain's supreme test. Only thus can the full force of his experience be borne home.

In the second place, January 1 was one of the most popular feast days, if not the most popular, of pagan Europe, and especially of Rome. So much is this the case that the Feast of the Circumcision, which entered the calendar rather late (sixth or perhaps fifth century), may have been instituted, in part, as Christian protest against the continuing celebration of pagan feasts.[3] Be that as it may, the Church did eventually counter pagan practices by the institution of a special office for New Year's Day, in addition to the Feast of the Circumcision, entitled—pointedly enough since Gawain is guilty of a kind of idolatry—"Ad prohibendum ab idolis" (Cabrol, DACL 3:2:1721). This appropriately two-faced characteristic of January 1 (Janus) continues even into the fourteenth century. In his sermon "De Circumcisione Domini nostri, Ihesu Christi," John Mirk informs his congregation that

> Hit ys callet New-3erys-day, for hit ys þe forme day of þe kalender. . . . Sayth Seynt Austeyn þat, þis day and þis nyght, paynene vsen mony fals opynyons of wychecraft and of fals fayth, *þe whech ben noght to telle among crysten men, lest þay wer drawen yn vse.* Wherefor, 3e þat ben Goddys seruandes, be 3e well war, lest 3e ben desyvet by any sorsery and by any byleue: *as by takyng of howsell of on man raythyr þen of anoþyr, othyr forto bye othyr selle, and aske or borue.* Yn þe whyche some men haue dyuerse opynyons þat, *3yf þay werne clene schereven, þay wer worthy gret penawnce for mysbeleue; for þat comyth of þe fende, and not of God.*[4]

Mirk also reminds his congregation that New Year's Day is to pass "*wythouten any new cownant makyng.* For a good seruand þat hath a good maystyr, he maketh but onys cownant wyth hym, but soo holdeth forth from 3ere to 3ere, *hauyng full tryst yn his maystyr þat he woll for his good seruyce reward at hys ende and at his nede*" (Mirk 1905:44; emphasis added). Now in addition to demonstrating the longevity of pagan feasts and customs, even into his own day ("whech ben noght to telle among crysten men, lest þay wer drawen yn vse"), Mirk's remarks also indicate the role of commerce in the lore of January 1; and they may, accordingly, bear directly on *Sir Gawain*. In particular, Mirk may help to explain why Gawain confesses right after receiving the girdle but before the third and final exchange with Bertilak.

After the Lady leaves the bedchamber for the third and last time, Gawain

> Rises and riches hym in araye noble,
> Lays vp þe luf-lace þe lady hym raȝt,
> Hid hit ful holdely, þer he hit eft fonde.
> Syþen cheuely to þe chapel choses he þe waye,
> Preuély aproched to a prest, and prayed hym þere
> Þat he wolde lyste his lyf and lern hym better
> How his sawle schulde be saued when he schuld seye heþen.
> Þere he schrof hym schyrly and schewed his mysdedez,
> Of þe more and þe mynne, and merci besechez,
> And of absolucioun he on þe segge calles:
> And he asoyled hym surely and sette hym so clene
> As domezday schulde haf ben diȝt on þe morn.
>
> (1873–84)

I have quoted at such length because this is such a difficult and important passage. Note, in particular, first, that Gawain *hides* the girdle— and apparently thinks nothing of it—and, second, that the priest absolves him completely. The text strongly suggests that Gawain is in a state of grace at this point. For this to be so, Gawain must have *schrof hym schyrly and schewed his mysdedez* in the conviction that concealing the girdle did *not* constitute a crime; otherwise, he would have had to confess it, and the priest, in turn, would have had to impose upon Gawain the 'satisfaction' (*satisfactio operis*) of returning the girdle.[5] Gawain could entertain such a conviction only by forgetting or refusing to regard the fact that he must soon exchange the girdle with Bertilak, at which time concealment would definitely constitute a crime, a breach of *couenaunt*. The question, then, is: why does he forget or ignore this fact?

Mirk's information is of great help now. Gawain may have believed that he was going to 'have commerce' (*bye othyr selle*) with the devil (recall Mirk's phrase, *þat comyth of þe fende*; and compare 2187–88 of the poem); if he did believe this, he might have gone to confession to ensure that he would be *clene schereven* when he met the devil (see 2188

Et procedens homo sine semine,
Largitus est nobis suam deitatem.[7]

O wonderful exchange, wonderful trade:
The Creator of human kind, assuming an inspirited body,
Deigned to be born of a Virgin;
And coming forth as a man without admixture of seed,
He bestowed upon us his godhead.

New Year's Day is the day of the 'admirable commerce' through which
the Maker of man exchanged his deity for his creature's body. On the
day when the Church celebrates the saving commerce of the *Deus-
Homo*, the Green Knight prices Gawain commercially.

Commentary on this antiphon begins at least as early as Amalarius
of Metz and remains remarkably consistent down through William
Durandus's *Rationale Divinorum Officiorum*.[8] In glossing *commercium*,
Amalarius (1948:507) notes that "quando dicit: commercium, ostendit
aliud dari, et aliud accipi. Dedit Christus suam deitatem, et accepit
nostram humanitatem. Quod dedit colimus in nativitate eius, et quod
accepit, in octavis (when the antiphon says 'commerce', it shows that
something is given and something received. Christ gave His deity and
received our humanity. What He gave we celebrate during the feast of
His nativity, and what He received, during that of the octave)." Just
so, on New Year's Day, the Octave of Christmas, at the Green Chapel,
Gawain *accepit nostram humanitatem*: he bleeds (2314). I am not sug-
gesting that Gawain is a Christ figure; the poem does not ask to be
read that way. But the poem is about a Christian knight and about one
whose *cowarddyse and couetyse* had blinded him to his humanity and
original culpability. To these the Green Knight opens his eyes again.
Having become *proud of þe prys* that Bertilak's Lady 'put on him,' Gawain fell victim to that *superbia vitae* (1 John 2. 16; Howard 1966:232–
35) because of which he *lufed* [his] *lyf* (2368) and therefore *lewté
wonted* (2366). The Green Knight blames him the less (2368) because
he loved his life *but* blames him still. For had Gawain, knight of the
Virgin Mary that he is (645–50), previously followed Christ without
reservation, he would have accepted *nostram humanitatem*, as did
Christ, unto the death (Phil. 2. 5–8). But there's the rub: it is difficult
for a mere man to follow Christ without reservation.

Of particular relevance here is an often repeated remark that origi-
nates with Amalarius (1948:507): "Christi adventum ad homines colimus in die nativitatis ejus: hominum adventum ad Christum colimus

in octavis eius (The advent of Christ to men we celebrate in the day of his nativity: the advent of man to Christ we celebrate on its octave, eight days later)." Extending and clarifying this formula, Sicard of Cremona adds: "*ipse autem venit ad nos, ut iremus ad eum,* et hoc ex antiphonis manifeste dignoscitur (He Himself came to us that we might go to Him, and this is clearly taught in the octave)" (PL 213:226; emphasis added). On the Feast of the Circumcision the Church celebrates the advent of man to Christ—"Largitus est nobis suam deitatem"—which is possible because of the advent of Christ to man— "animatum corpus sumens, / De Virgine nasci dignatus est." Christ bought our humanity and paid his deity for it: this was the exchange —"egit enim in cruce grande commercium" (see chap. 1 at n. 7). The order of events is important here. Man becomes God only because God became man; man comes to Christ only because Christ came to man—"ipse autem venit ad nos, ut iremus ad eum." Or, as St. Augustine, whom Amalarius (1948:506) quotes, puts it (*De Doctrina Christiana,* CCSL 32:12):

Non enim ad eum, qui ubique praesens est, locis movetur, sed bono studio bonisque moribus. Quod non possumus, nisi ipsa sapientia tantae etiam nostrae infirmitati congruere dignaretur, ut vivendi nobis praeberet exemplum. Non enim aliter, quam in homine, quoniam et nos homines sumus.

For to Him who is everywhere present there is no approach through places but through good endeavor and good customs. Such approaches we cannot make unless Wisdom Himself deigns to participate in so many of our ills and weaknesses that He might offer an example to us living men. For such an example is not otherwise available to us than in a man since we too are men.

Had not Christ become the Son of Man, men could not become the sons of God. Full acceptance of *nostram humanitatem,* therefore, in the manner of Christ, is necessary to receiving the largesse of deity ("largitus est nobis suam deitatem").[9] The error of Gawain, however, is to have refused *nostram humanitatem* where Christ fully accepted it, unto death. Gawain will not, as every man eventually must, lay his life down. Who of us can blame him? He accepts the green girdle to save his life. So would we. But in doing so, he exchanges his *prys* for his life; he pays for his life with his *prys.* But, as he soon learns, without his *prys* his life is precisely worthless. Gawain's refusal of *nostram hu-*

manitatem, his fear of death or his belief that he must live at all costs, finally surprises and disheartens *him* more than anyone else. He should have known better:

> 'Corsed worth cowarddyse and couetyse boþe!
> In yow is vylany and vyse þat vertue disstryez.'
> Þenne he kaȝt to þe knot, and þe kest lawsez,
> Brayde broþely þe belt to þe burne seluen;
> 'Lo! þer þe falssyng, foule mot hit falle,
> For care of þy knokke cowardyse me taȝt
> To acorde me with couetyse, my kynde to forsake,
> Þat is larges and lewté þat longez to knyȝtez.
> Now am I fawty and falce, and ferde haf ben euer
> Of trecherye and vntrawþe.'
>
> (2374–83)

And it surprises and disheartens him so because he has been long deceived about his own humanity. A member of Arthur's court, where the king himself is *childgered* (86) and *wylde* of *brayn* (89), Gawain— like his king, flushed with youth, "for al watz þis fayre folk in her first age" (54)—had taken it for granted that he was the ideal knight, just as Arthur's was the ideal court (cf. Blenkner 77:379–80; Burrow 1965:50–51). He had presumed upon a *nurture* as yet untested, untried. Because of that presumption and because of that untried *nurture*, Gawain did not really *know*, however easily he might have been able to name, what his *kynde* was. Ignorant and inexperienced, he had assumed, so his behavior suggests, that *larges and lewté* would follow naturally upon being a knight. But it is not so simple as that, he finally learns. A man and his *kynde* are not necessarily one, especially when his *kynde* is *larges and lewté*. Both terms are crucial but *larges* has pride of place and for good reason if we think of the antiphon. For *larges is* the *kynde*—"largitus est nobis suam deitatem"—of the truest *miles* or Christ.[10] And Gawain could never have lived up to this *kynde*. He could never have been so generous as to lay down his life, as did the *miles* Christ. And this because he is human. Both he and Arthur had ignored, as youths inevitably do, that they are only human. Gawain had ignored the flesh and the flesh's weakness—"'þe faute and þe fayntyse of þe flesche crabbed, / How tender hit is to entyse teches of fylþe'" (2435–56)—and this is why his flesh overwhelms him with the love of life when the Lady presents him with the girdle. Gawain had not really thought about death yet, even though he had been taking thought for it ever since setting out from Arthur's court.

To pursue the same line of reasoning further: having resisted the Lady's previous sexual advances, Gawain has, by the time she shows him the girdle, triumphed heroically over the flesh. If he has experienced the weakness of the flesh, he has also overcome it. And in the wake of this triumph must come—it is hard to imagine it otherwise—pride in its achievement (*superbia vitae*). And this self-congratulatory pride—the pride of, so to say, "Yes, I *am* an honorable knight"—undermines Gawain's defenses when the Lady tempts him at last not with sexual desire but with the far more powerful, instinctual, and uncontrollable desire to live. Gregory the Great (PL 76:453; emphasis added) very aptly describes Gawain's predicament in his discussion, not inappropriately, of circumcision:

Alia est luxuria carnis qua castitatem corrumpimus, alia vero *luxuria cordis est qua de castitate gloriamur*. Dicitur ergo [God to Job] "Accinge sicut vir lumbos tuos" [Job 38.3], *ut qui prius luxuriam corruptionis vicerat*, nunc luxuriam restringat elationis, *ne de patientia vel castitate superbiens*, tanto pejus intus ante Dei oculos luxuriosus existeret, *quanto magis ante oculos hominum et patiens et castus appareret*. Unde bene per Moysen dicitur: "Circumcidite praeputia cordis vestri" (Deut. 10. 16), id est, *postquam luxuriam a carne exstinguitis, etiam superflua cogitationum resecate*.

There is one kind of lust, namely of the flesh, by which we corrupt chastity, another, however, namely of the heart, by which we glory in our chastity. Hence God says to Job: "Gird up your loins like a man" [Job 38. 3], so that whoever first conquers the lust of corruption may now restrain the lust of glorying, lest becoming proud of his patience and chastity, he live so much the worse lustful within, before the eyes of God, as he appears the more both patient and chaste, before the eyes of man. Hence well is it said by Moses: 'Circumcise the foreskin of your hearts' (Deut. 10. 16), that is, after you douse the lust arising from the flesh, cut off also the excesses of thought and imagination.

Although Gawain has, in fact, achieved a brilliant appearance of patience and chastity before the Lady—and thus, at least as he sees it, before the world, too—he is *not* as yet circumcised in heart. And so, *de patientia vel castitate superbiens*, he accepts the girdle which, as a *syngne of surfet*, suggests that, in part at least, his error has been one, in Gregory's words, of *superflua cogitationum*. Moreover, in accepting the girdle, his *superflua cogitationum* extend to an oath of secrecy and thus to treachery. Hence Gawain's triumph over the flesh, his very idealism of chivalric duty, weakens his resistance to the flesh and its many temptations. And so it is that the Green Knight finally leaves Gawain with not only knowledge of the weight of the flesh but also with the humility to acknowledge his own foolish pride. Gawain declares:

> 'Bot in syngne of my surfet I schal se hit ofte,
> When I ride in renoun, remorde to myseluen
> Þe faut and þe fayntyse of þe flesche crabbed,
> How tender hit is to entyse teches of fylþe;
> And þus, quen *pryde* schal me pryk for prowes of armes,
> Þe loke to þis luf-lace schal leþe my hert.'
> (lines 2433–38: emphasis added)

When the Green Knight *prices* Gawain—when he *comparat militem Arthuri*[11]—on this day of *admirabile commercium*, he reminds Gawain of that exchange, that commerce, between *Deus* and *Homo*, between deity *and* humanity, between spirit *and* flesh, which in his youthful idealism he had ignored. Although Gawain is a superior man, he is still a man, not yet a deity, and therefore he is still subject to the marketplace of this world where the commerce between deity and humanity goes on. When Gawain looks hereafter to the *syngne of surfet*, he will see the weight of the flesh and thus also that concupiscence which is the *reatus* of original sin.[12] He will never again be so proud as to forget that he is only human.

Now the consequences of the Green Knight's circumcision of Gawain justify this claim: "'I halde þe polysed of þat plyȝt, and pured as clene / As þou hadez neuer forfeted syþen þou watz fyrst borne'" (2393–94). Restoration of Gawain to the innocence (albeit self-conscious) of infancy is just what we should expect from the circumcision because it is a rite precisely of canceling the debt of *peccatum originale*. As a Feast of the Octave, or Eighth Day, the Feast of the Circumcision, according to Sicard of Cremona (PL 213:227), celebrates renovation and regeneration:

> Est demum omnium octavarum ratio generalis, quod octava redit ad caput. . . . Idem quoque dies primus est et octavus, id est Dominicus. Ideoque resurrectio Domini dicitur facta in octava, id est in die Dominica. Idcirco igitur observatur celebritas octavarum, ut revertamur ad primum innocentiae statum; in cujus innocentiae recordatione, in octava die Circumcisio agebatur, ut mens circumcisa fieret ab omni carnali contagione.

In fact, the general explanation of every octave is this, that it returns to the beginning. . . . The first day and the eighth day are exactly the same—that is, Sunday. Thus the resurrection of the Lord is said to have taken place on the octave, that is, on the day of the Lord, Sunday. On this account, therefore, the celebration of the octave is observed, that we might return to the first state of innocence; and in commemoration of this innocence, on the eighth day, circumcision was performed, so that the mind might be circumcised or cut off from all carnal contamination.

Circumcising Gawain by the nick on the neck, the Green Knight ultimately renews in him the effects of baptism: "Circumcisio carnis, lege praecepta est; qua non posset melius significari, per Christum regenerationis auctorem tolli originale peccatum (Circumcision of the flesh is a precept of the Law; this precept signifies nothing so clearly as the taking away of original sin [i.e., baptism] by Christ, the author of regeneration)" (St. Augustine, PL 45:1173). Circumcision, like baptism, *tollit originale peccatum*. Hence the precision of the poem's words: "'as þou hadez neuer *forfeted* syþen þou watz *fyrst* borne'" (emphasis added). Gawain was first born of the flesh from his mother's womb. He was born again, a second birth, of the waters of baptism, when the coin of his soul was stamped with the character of the sacrament that removes original sin.[13]

A pause is necessary here to quarrel with the T-G-D edition which glosses *forfet* as 'transgress'. This is in error. If *forfet* meant 'transgress', the Green Knight would be saying, "as though you had never transgressed or sinned from the time of your first birth." No Christian sacrament has this effect. Rather, baptism, like circumcision, can only take away the penalty, the fine, the punishment—the forfeiture (or guilt)—for original sin.[14] Neither baptism nor circumcision can take away the effects of original sin, namely concupiscence and ignorance.[15] Concupiscence and ignorance remain, and, because they remain, men continue to sin. The Green Knight, therefore, has no authority to say that Gawain has never sinned. But he does have the authority to say precisely, "as though you had never paid the fine or the forfeiture from the time of your first birth," because circumcision, like baptism, remits the penalty of original sin retroactively from the moment of carnal birth and ever thereafter. Hence Gawain will continue to sin, as all men do because of *þe faut and þe fayntyse of þe flesche crabbed*, but the Green Knight has renewed, or celebrated again, Gawain's redemption from the debt or fine of his sin—which of course has been debited to the account of Christ, *agnus Dei qui tollit peccata mundi*. The doctrinal precision of the poem's commercial imagery is no mean part of its extraordinary beauty.

Equally impressive is the extent of the emphasis on regeneration and renovation in the poem. When Gawain first flinches from the ax, the Green Knight exclaims, "'Þou art not Gawayn'" (2270) as if he would unname Arthur's knight. But after Gawain has accepted *nostram humanitatem* by shedding his blood in the circumcision, the Green Knight renames him:

> 'and sothly me þynkkez
> On þe fautlest freke þat euer on fote ȝede;
> As perle bi þe quite pese is of prys more,
> So is Gawayn, in god fayth, bi oþer gay knyȝtez.'
>   (2362–65)

Although the name is the same, in the second *impositio*—which is commercial and comparative, fully mediatory—it is nonetheless new. As in fact it should be, according to Sicard (PL 213:227), following as it does the rite of circumcision:

> De circumcisione et nominis impositione sermo succedat, et merito in octavo die circumcisionis, et nominis, quod est Jesus, impositionis solemnitas celebratur.

> Concerning the circumcision and the imposition of the name, the discourse continues; and rightly on the eighth day is celebrated the rite of the circumcision and of the imposition of the name, which is Jesus.

The Feast of the Circumcision is also the celebration of the imposition of the name Jesus which, as commentators emphasize, is the *novum nomen*.[16] Similarly, though he may not receive literally a new name, Gawain receives his name anew; and in this sense, his name *is* new —gratuitously imposed and not achieved, a gift he could not have earned by any knightly deed. And Gawain accepts his name, for the first time, even as he accepts *nostram humanitatem* for the first time. Gawain is renewed in the *admirabile commercium* that the Feast of the Circumcision celebrates.

If *Sir Gawain and the Green Knight* is doctrinally precise, it is not, of course, precisely doctrinal. It is a poem, not a treatise, and is accordingly not restricted to expository logic. Hence, for example, the significance of the Feast of the Circumcision figures within the larger context of the sacrament of penitence that is fundamental to the poem's structure. In "'þe corsedest kyrk þat euer [he] com inne'" (2196), Gawain meets a confessor of sorts who shrives and absolves him (Burrow 1965:127–33). The poem adds circumcision to penitence, to draw imagery from them both, because, in part, as its relation to baptism suggests, circumcision is a kind of penitence for original sin: it is a *satisfaction* in and of the flesh, a payment by the body, of the fine Adam incurred. Moreover, circumcision, like penitence, is an ascesis of the senses. Numerous exegetes agree with Honorius Augustodunensis that "circumcisio Domini ideo agitur, ut et nos spiritualiter circumcidamur quinque sensibus nostris (Circumcision of the Lord is thus celebrated, so that we too will be circumcised spiritually in our five senses)." [17] The circumcision or ascesis of the five senses is an image of considerable importance to *Sir Gawain* since, first of all, one of the five points of the pentangle signifies that Gawain *watz funden fautlez in his fyue wyttez* (640) and since, second, when Gawain first arrives at the *corsed kyrk*, he complains, "'Now I fele hit is þe fende in my fyue wyttez, / Þat hatz stoken me þis steuen to strye me here'" (2193–94). Supposedly faultless in his five senses, Gawain in fact suffers deceit because of and through them: it is through his *fyue wyttez*, especially the *wyt* of hearing, that Bertilak's Lady persuades him to break his covenant with his host; and the same *wyttez* suggest to him, quite erroneously, that it is the fiend who had lured him to the Green Chapel. Obviously, then, Gawain's senses are in need of the circumcision that they eventually receive at the hands of the Green Knight. Circumcised and purified at last, they will enable him, in his repentance, to remember and celebrate what he should never have forgotten, the *admirabile commercium* of the *Deus-Homo*.

iii. *Sacramentum Mediatoris in carne venturi*

The sacramentality of the rite of circumcision is as important to *Sir Gawain and the Green Knight* as the liturgy of the Feast of the Circumcision because it is an important element in the Christian theory of signification and mediation. Burrow (1965:187–89) has rightly emphasized the unusual extent to which *Sir Gawain* concerns itself with signs and signification. This concern reflects controversies that had been underway for at least a century, and in certain respects for much longer than that, both in theology and philosophy, especially the philosophy of language. From a very wide perspective, the principal controversy is that ancient one between convention, *nomos*, and nature, *physis* (Manley 1980:54–65). From a narrower perspective, restricted to the thirteenth and fourteenth centuries, it centers in the two distinct but related questions of sacramental causality and of the origins of words and their meanings. At this point we are primarily concerned with the first of these questions and *Sir Gawain*'s reflection of it.

Christianity's theory, or perhaps we should say theories, of signification and mediation were hardly static at any time in its history, but they were undergoing seminal change in the thirteenth and fourteenth centuries as theologians probed the mystery of sacramental causality.[18] Some, Aquinas for example, argued that the sacraments of the New Covenant *efficiunt quod significant* ("effect what they signify") because of value inherent in them.[19] Other theologians, notably Franciscans like Bonaventure and nominalists like Pierre d'Ailly, argued that the sacraments were thus efficacious because of value ascribed to them by God through his covenant (*pactum*) with man: in the words of William Courtenay (1971:119), "*de potentia ordinata* . . . the sacraments effect grace *ex pacto*, that is, they operate within and because of God's ordained system, his covenant with the Church. . . . Theological causation, *de potentia ordinata*, is . . . exclusively *ex pacto* or *sine qua non* . . . in the sense that man's merit or the sacraments are signs or tokens that will unfailingly and directly produce their effect because God has committed himself to accord such a value to them." Courtenay and Oberman, among others, have remarked on the extraordinary importance to this shift in theory of contemporary economic change and upheaval:

> Behind the initial argument for *sine qua non* causality and Thomas's rejection of it lay two conflicting theories of monetary value within a metallistic system. One theory, supported by Thomas and dominant throughout the Middle Ages, maintained that money must consist of a precious metal or other substance having, because of its composition, a value equivalent to the commodities for which it is exchanged, allowance being made for shifts in market value as a result of supply and demand. The second theory, appearing toward the middle of the thirteenth century and distrusted by Thomas, maintained that money need not "consist of" but need only be "covered by" a commodity having value apart from its monetary role. (Courtenay 1972: 188)

Oberman's incisive characterization (1977:167) also deserves quotation:

> Die von Duns Scotus entwickelte und von den Nominalisten übernommene Akzeptationslehre—die Rechtfertigung durch Gottes

"Annahme" der an und für sich ungenügenden menschlichen Gerechtigkeit—findet eine deutliche Parallele in dem *valor extrinsecus*, d.h. in dem zugeschriebenen Wert des Geldes.

The acceptation doctrine, developed by Duns Scotus and taken up too by the nominalists—the doctrine, in other words, that man's righteousness, insufficient in and of itself, is justified by God's "acceptance" of it—finds a clear parallel in the concept of *valor extrinsecus*, that is, in the concept of the ascribed value of money.

It is in such an economic and theological context as this that *Sir Gawain and the Green Knight*, a poem concerned with covenants (*pacta*) if ever there was one, explores the margin between signs and sacraments. The poem moves from a theory of inherent value, evinced chiefly in the pentangle, to a theory of ascribed value, evinced chiefly in the green girdle. Youthful idealists, like the folk who inhabit Arthur's court (54), believe quite readily in the inherent value of human signs, such as pentangles and chivalric manners. It seems characteristic of youth to take such things very seriously. Mature stewards of the ideal, however, such as the humbled and circumcised Gawain, accept that all signs of human institution are arbitrary, relative, comparative, ascriptive. Youthful idealists (*childgered* and of *brayn wylde*) are particularly vulnerable to idolatry because of their devotion to the inherent value of signs; mature stewards of the ideal are much less vulnerable, without necessarily being cynical, since they can recognize the arbitrariness of a value without mocking the value. Mature stewards of the ideal know that all signs are separated from their signified by the distance of their arbitrary institution; at the same time, however, they also know that this distance does not necessarily preclude faith in the possibility of meaning. Moreover, in addition to such faith is an exception to the rule of arbitrary institution: namely, those signs that are sacraments by virtue of the *pactum* that God made with man through His only begotten Son. These signs, as sacraments, *efficiunt quod significant*. The mature steward of the ideal, then, is neither cynic nor infidel. He is, rather, someone who recognizes the quandary of the ideal—an absolute that is nonetheless arbitrary. He is someone who, in the poem's sense of things, has been circumcised.

Circumcision constitutes a very special case of sacramentality, one that is directly relevant to *Sir Gawain*'s narrative motion from a theory of inherent to a theory of ascriptive value. Circumcision is a sacrament instituted *ante legem* and operative *sub lege* (see chap. 2 at n. 6). It is not a sacrament of the new *pactum* but a sacrament of the old *pactum*. As such it is the *sacramentum Mediatoris in carne venturi* ("sacrament of the Mediator who is [yet] *to come* in the flesh").[20] Circumcision in the flesh of Abraham and his seed is a sign and a sign *only* of their *faith* in the Mediator to come.[21] Therefore, circumcision is the sacrament that retains and makes visible the essential differentiae of the sign: it is radically separated from its signified—*in carne venturi*—and it remains the presence of an absence—a mark or a trace in the flesh, of a reality absent temporally and materially (cf. Saussure 1966:123). Circumcision is a sacrament or rite, therefore, openly significatory and mediatory; as such, it is the rite through which Gawain the youthful idealist is finally instructed in the mature understanding and thus stewardship of signs and ideals. Circumcision is a rite that emphasizes the separateness of sign and signified; just so, Gawain, who had collapsed the ideal that he signified into identity with his own person, its sign, is circumcised so as to emerge from the ritual wearing a sign, the *syngne of surfet* and *token of vntrawpe* which is a wisp of cloth indisputably separate from its signified. Gawain's error was finally the error of idolatry, the deliberate confusion of sign and signified. He is liberated from his error and purified through a rite or sacrament that was instituted, Aquinas tells us, against idolatry.[22]

Sir Gawain and the Green Knight was composed in a world that had restored to rightful eminence in human thought the radical Otherness of God who, still, from that Otherness, covenants with man to love and cherish him. The poem was composed in a world where the armor of Platonic idealism had begun to show chinks. It was composed in a world where signification had become just one more human institution contingent upon the benevolence of the Holy Other. From such a world, the poem gathered a vision of faith—faith as fragile and as delicate as the media that exchange it between man and man, between man and God. For such a world, the poem figures in the circumcision of Gawain the restoration of mediation and faith to the court of Arthur, the return of the *admirabile commercium* of the Mediator whose birth that court was celebrating the day the Green Knight cried, "'Wher is . . . / Þe gouernour of þis gyng?'" (224–25).

3

Love's Relations:
The Seduction of Gawain

i. The Case against *Surquidré*

It will be helpful at this point to take stock of the argument and to anticipate later positions. If we have just grounded the commercial vocabulary in its contemporary context, we have as yet to read that vocabulary in its text. If the theology, the liturgy, and the sacramentality of circumcision help to isolate *Sir Gawain*'s vision of relativity, relationships, and mediation in human society, that vision is fully available only in the text and particularly in those moments of the text in which the commercial vocabulary dominates. The sum of those moments describes a process of commercialization which goes, in brief, something like this.

In his youthful idealism and unreflective devotion to knighthood, Gawain has misunderstood the role of relativity and relationship in human affairs. At the center of this misunderstanding is an ill-considered presumption, if considered at all, of the inherent value of things. In the poem's language, Gawain is guilty of *surquidré* (311, 2457) or that pride that inhibits the necessary questioning and probing of the value of things. As the exemplar of Arthur's court (see 911–23), Gawain believes that his *nurture* is an absolute standard of civilization by which to measure and to rule human achievement. But the measure must be measured. It is the Green Knight's express business "'to assay þe surquidré, ȝif hit soth were / Þat rennes of þe grete renoun of þe Rounde Table'" (2457–58). *Assay*, with its emphasis on measuring and weighing, is of course a crucial term of the commerical vocabulary and of the vision that emerges from it. As crucial, though less insistent, is *rennes*. If word (whether *soth* or false) of the renown of the Round Table *runs* (see 310, where the same point is made), then renown is subject to the circulation in that running. And this is consistent with the nature of renown: being eminently a matter of words, it is dependent on relativity. It must be related from one source to another, and its value is relative to the standards of those who receive it. Renown, then, is a kind of currency, and when the poem uses *rennes* it acknowledges as much. Moreover, it also suggests, though obliquely, that renown, like currency, has an exchange rate; and, for example, at Hautdesert, *nurture* is not worth quite so much as it is at Camelot: though highly *praysed* at first, its *prys* eventually suffers deflation.

But Gawain is ignorant of all this when he first arrives, still untested. To correct this state of affairs, the Green Knight and those in collaboration with him bring about Gawain's exposure to the inevitable relativity and contingency of human intercourse: they help him to see that he is human, therefore incomplete and in need of relationships—in need of others and of their views and of the humility that can accept them. They show him that value is not inherent in things so much as it is ascribed to things by human subjectivity (a fact not unknown, perhaps, but conveniently forgotten at Camelot). Thus, for example, Gawain subjectively values the green girdle as worth his life and therefore his *lewté*. But his testers do not abandon him to conclude from his behavior that individual subjectivity is the sole arbiter of value. Rather they help him to see that if the extreme of unreflective *surquidré* is a sin, such as besets Arthur's court where relations have ossified into formality, so also is the opposite extreme of insistence on private value to the exclusion of relations, such as he lapses into under the pressure of his fear of beheading. The latter, in fact, is as much *surquidré* as the former. Thus Gawain learns not only that formality is a biased determinant of value but also that the relativity of all goods does not mean that all value is solely subjective.

Quite the contrary, value is a function of convention, itself a force of human community and concert—hence the common value of the green girdle when Gawain returns to Arthur's court. But Gawain does not understand the conventionality of values because of his idealistic and unexamined assumption of his own *nurture* as *the* standard. Whether at Camelot or Hautdesert, Gawain relies on formality, the formality emerging from his *nurture*: he assumes he can behave his way out of any situation, and this assumption is based on the prior assumption that his values are intact and absolute. But the purpose of the *gomen* at Bertilak's castle is to fix Gawain and his values in situations where they cannot remain intact and absolute. He is soon to see that other people value things and people in other ways. And this is the first step toward his mature stewardship of the ideals that he embodies. The mature steward of the ideal understands that every good is a created good and therefore a medium to and vestigium of its Creator, God. So much is a datum of the Augustinian environment in

which *Sir Gawain and the Green Knight* was composed (see chap. 1 at nn.
5 and 6). For him, then, the value of every good is relative to, ultimately, its greater or lesser manifestation of the Creator: it refers to
the Creator. Because of this reference, any construction of the value
of a created good must begin in love of the Creator. One may not
know the value of some good, for whatever reason, but if one loves
the Creator of that good, one will not misuse it. Moreover, and very
importantly, by loving the Creator of that good, one will be naturally
disposed to loving others with whom one must decide on its value.
One will be willing to work toward some agreement about its value.
The mature steward of the ideal recognizes that all created goods—
and ideals are, of course, created goods—must be valued in and with
love of the Creator and the community or risk being undervalued or
overvalued. Usually, it is in the direction of overvaluing that men,
being men, err. And when this happens, a created good tends to replace or at least to obscure its Creator. In terms of its status as sign,
this created good displaces its signified or supplements its signified so
as to replace it; and the result is idolatry. Gawain, we shall see, is guilty
of idolatry—of letting his service to the ideal of the pentangle become
his sole concern—because of his youthful idealism that motivates him
to serve the ideal so passionately and that drives him to incarnate it so
completely. To renounce his idolatry without abandoning his idealism,
Gawain must attain some distance on the ideal, some maturity.

The mature steward of the ideal is mature because he questions
even the value of the ideal; he recognizes that pride can also insinuate
itself where one is most careful against it. In Gawain's case, this vulnerable spot is the pentangle, and to be a mature steward of the ideal
it represents, he must beware of the pride it might and did inspire. In
fact, this is what he promises the Green Knight he will do:

'And þus, quen *pryde* schal me pryk for prowes of armes,
Þe loke to þis luf-lace schal leþe my hert.'
(2437–38; emphasis added)

I think we can assume that the shield *cum* pentangle and portrait of
Mary (646–50) represents *prowes of armes*—certainly this is consonant
with the nature of a shield—and if we do, we can see that these two
lines balance and oppose the shield (in 2437) and the green girdle,
or the *luf-lace* (in 2438). Gawain is saying, in effect, that the object
through which he learned humility, the *luf-lace*, will henceforth chasten the pride that the shield and the ideal it represents inspired in
him. Gawain will henceforth be a mature steward of the ideal because

he will appreciate from now on the relative value of all ideals—their conventionality.

And this he will be able to do because the Green Knight has *priced* him in the 'admirable commerce' of circumcision, itself an element of the divine economy. Once he has priced him, the Green Knight goes on to absolve Gawain who will never again, out of *surquidré*, presume to master the ideal. Rather, hereafter he will wear a sign, wear it as a kind of retribution (as well as a badge of honor) because it is incomplete, relative, and mediate. Moreover, at the end of his adventure (and the poem) he has returned to laughter, the very music of the human condition of relativity, in which laughter Arthur's court *luflyly acorden* (2514)—that is, establish a convention—to share his sign in a triumph, however fleeting, of mature love for, not love of, this *bonum, valde bonum* world.

ii. What *Prys* Gawain?

The lesson that Gawain learns at Hautdesert is this: that his *prys* and his *cost(es)* are not definitive, nor are they the measure; rather, they are *to be* defined, they are *to be* measured. When the members of the household at Hautdesert discover, on Gawain's first night with them, who it is that they are entertaining, they react like fans hailing an "idol." They are overjoyed to have *fonged þat fyne fader of nurture* in whom they expect to see—as if he were the entertainer and they the audience—"'sleȝtez of þewez / And þe teccheles termes of talkyng noble / [And] wich spede is in speche'" (916–18). Of course, such a fan club must flatter any man, but it presents him with a predicament, too. In fact, Gawain's fan club defines the predicament that he faces throughout his stay at Hautdesert:

> And alle þe men in þat mote maden much joye
> To apere in his presense prestly þat tyme,
> Þat alle *prys* and prowes and pured þewes
> Apendes to hys persoun, and *praysed* is euer;
> Byfore alle men vpon molde his mensk is þe most.
> (910–14; emphasis added)

Although *prys* in this context chiefly suggests its Old French sense of 'excellence' or 'nobility', the primary sense of 'price' (*pretium*) is hardly absent, especially since the context emphasizes Gawain's presence, his show, or theater. Gawain's *prys*—excellence and price—depends on

the repute that his fans accord him unquestioningly: they appraise
him as well as praise him.[1] The *prys* belongs to (*apendes to*) Gawain, but
his possession of it is obviously inseparable from the fans who pay his
prys, who exchange their adulation for his theater, who are sold on
and sold by his goods. A later passage of the poem emphasizes this
fact also. On her first visit to his bedroom, Bertilak's Lady takes pains
to suggest to Gawain that he has, as it were, advance billing to live
up to:

'For I wene wel, iwysse, Sir Wowen ʒe are,
Þat alle þe worlde worchipez quere-so ʒe ride;
Your honour, your hendelayk is hendely *praysed*
With lordez, wyth ladyes, with alle þat lyf bere.
And now ʒe ar here, iwysse, and we bot oure one. . . .'
                                        (1226–30; emphasis added)

It follows from Gawain's dependence on an audience that he must sell
his fans by displaying or advertising his *þewes*, his *teccheles termes of
talkyng noble*, his craft of *luf-talkyng*. And it is precisely this display that
must begin to press upon Gawain an awareness of the relativity of values: to fetch a good price—that is, to win a noble *prys*—Gawain must
be solicitous of his image. He must become conscious of himself as a
commodity in (so to speak) the market of chivalric manners. Gawain
serves as all good(s) to all consumers; and this is, he eventually learns,
to risk being nothing.

The risk emerges starkly during the temptation scenes. The irony
of Gawain's predicament during these scenes, especially since he will
finally go to the length of insisting on an exclusively private value, lies
in his proud naïveté in matters mercantile because of which Bertilak's
Lady succeeds in seducing him. For example, in the second temptation scene, when Gawain fails to kiss the Lady, she lightly chides him
and declares that he cannot "*of compaynye þe costez vndertake*" (1483).
Although *costez* may well mean 'manners' here, as the T-G-D edition
suggests (1967:173), it also means, in the commercial system of the
poem, 'cost'. And as the event all too clearly proves, Gawain indeed
cannot undertake, he cannot manage, the *cost* of this Lady's company.
So far from it, in fact, that her company will cost him his *lewté* and
trawþe.

In the first temptation scene, Bertilak's Lady introduces Gawain to
the relativity of *prys*—its contingency upon a market of intricate and
largely invisible relations—by beginning with overt seduction:

'And syþen I haue in þis hous hym þat al lykez,
I schal ware my whyle wel, quyl hit lastez,
　　　with tale.
　　3e ar welcum to my cors,
　　Yowre awen won to wale,
　　Me behouez of fyne force
　　Your seruaunt be, and schale.'
　　　　　　(1234–40)

Bertilak's Lady may be subtle, but she is by no means shy (cf. Burrow
1965:80–82). Although a double entendre in line 1236 is almost
certainly to be excluded, irony there certainly is at the expense of
fin'amors in the phrase *fyne force.*[2] And this irony, combined with the
general tone of polite but nonetheless insistent flattery, serves to at-
tack Gawain's self-image at just that point of nobility and courtesy
where he would think himself the most scrupulous. Understandably,
then, he squirms a bit here:

'In god fayth,' quoþ Gawayn, 'gayn hit me þynkkez,
Þa3 I be not now he þat 3e of speken;
To reche to such reuerence as 3e reherce here
I am wy3e vnworþy, I wot wel myseluen.'
　　　　　　(1241–44; emphasis added)

Of course, he, Gawain, would never presume to take such advantage
as the Lady suggests. But this assertion of character is a subversion of
identity. In having to distinguish his "Gawain" from the Lady's "Gawain"—"'I be not now he þat 3e of speken'"—Gawain must face,
quite abruptly, the fact that he is not his own, that someone else can
lay claim to his identity in a world of relative values. Gawain is subject
to a pricing he can only partially control—which lends considerable
irony, by the way, to his formulaic, unreflective *gayn hit me þynkkez.* He
and his name no longer form an easy identity as they did in the static,
hierarchical world of Arthur's court. In his evaluation of himself,
which is more a reflex of manners than of commercial understanding,
Gawain is *worth* less than he is in the Lady's evaluation of him. If he
really did 'know well himself' (and what he is saying), Gawain might
recognize that being worthier in the Lady's estimate really is to be unworthy in his own (*I am wy3e vnworþy*), for just such evaluations as this
will enable her to seduce him away from his "'kynde / . . . Þat is larges
and lewté þat longez to kny3tez'" (2381). If Gawain understood how

his name could be worthier than, could have more value than, he himself, he perhaps could avoid the coming trials of relativity and relationships.

But, as it is, Gawain is enmeshed in the market and the marketability of chivalric manners. He is speaking the Lady's language:

> 'Bi God, I were glad, and yow god þoȝt,
> At saȝe oþer at seruyce þat I sette myȝt
> To þe plesaunce of your prys—hit were a pure ioye.'
>
> (1245–47)

Although this is compressed and elliptical language, it can be expanded, with the exception of one phrase, without too much difficulty: "By God, I would be glad if it seemed good to you—I mean, it would be a pure joy—if I might do something or other, in word or deed, which would be"—but here is the exceptional phrase—*to þe plesaunce of your prys*. On the interpretation of *prys* and of the referent of *your prys* must depend any understanding of Gawain's self-image at this moment.

The T-G-D edition (1967:205) asks the reader to understand the phrase *your prys* as a polite expression for 'you', and doubtless some such meaning is applicable. But given the numerous occurrences in the poem of the word *prys* and the energy that they release, it is hardly likely that the meaning of the phrase excludes or dismisses the meaning of the word *prys*.

Now the word *prys* must mean here something like 'evaluation' or 'estimate' or 'esteem'; and the phrase '*to þe plesaunce of your prys*'—with the word so interpreted—something like 'the satisfaction of your esteem'. This much I imagine no one would quarrel with. The real question is, the satisfaction of your esteem of *whom*? Certainly, 'the satisfaction of your self-esteem' seems not only an obvious but also a very applicable meaning. Gawain would then be saying something like "I would be glad to be able to do something that would satisfy your sense of your worth, your sense of what you deserve." But this apparently obvious meaning—to adopt which, one must assume that Gawain is simply being polite—suppresses another, different meaning that emerges from the commercial rhetoric of the whole context. Gawain, his image of himself disturbed by his embarrassment at failing to live up to the Lady's image of him, could also be saying: "I would be glad to be able to do something that would satisfy your esteem, estimation or evaluation *of me*—something that would satisfy your *prys*/pricing of me." Gawain could be saying, "I would be glad to conform to the price you set on me" just as later he does say, "'I am proude of þe prys þat ȝe put on me'" (1277).

If Gawain is saying something like this—almost letting it slip out through his convoluted, elliptical syntax—it marks a sliding, however slight, into a state of mind dominated by the relativity of *prys* and its contingency on a market. This, in its turn, marks a considerable degree of success in the Lady's campaign: she is out to undermine Gawain's proud defenses against human incompleteness by maneuvering him into the experience of relativity, of being weighed and measured; and so far, so good. That Gawain *is* experiencing relativity here and that the Lady *is* succeeding in her part of the complicated *gomen* to humble Arthur's proud knight is confirmed by her immediate reply to his convoluted courtesy:

'In god fayth, Sir Gawayn,' quoþ þe gay lady,
'Þe *prys* and þe prowes þat plesez al oþer,
If I hit lakked oþer set at lyȝt, hit were littel daynté;
Bot hit ar ladyes innoȝe þat leuer wer nowþe
Haf þe, hende, in hor holde, as I þe habbe here,
To daly with derely your daynté wordez,
Keuer hem comfort and colen her carez,
Þen much of þe garysoun oþer golde þat þay hauen.'
                                   (1248–55; emphasis added)

Bertilak's Lady pounces on Gawain's use of *prys* since it plays right into her hands. And her answer presumes that Gawain said, "the satisfaction of your (the Lady's) esteem of me (Gawain)" because that is the statement to which it objects. It is as if she had said: "No, no, not *my prys* of you, but the *prys . . . þat plesez al oþer*—who am I to fault the market *prys* of Gawain, paragon of knights, all things to all women who, to be where I am, would pay out all the wealth that they own?" (see, further, 1228–33). Gawain *did* say, as far as Bertilak's Lady is concerned, "I would be glad to do something to the satisfaction of your esteem of me"; this we know because she instantly objects that *her prys* of Gawain is only the market *prys*, thus capitalizing on the opportunity to sweeten her flattery all the more. She maneuvers with extraordinary wit to keep Gawain's *prys* uppermost in his mind. In so doing, she constrains him to attend exclusively to her salesmanship and her pricing, so that she can gradually convince him that she is a shrewd judge of knight's flesh. She is measuring Gawain—he is worth his weight in the gold of all the women who desire him—and as she reduces him to a commodity, she not only convinces him that she is a sharp salesman, she also manipulates him into speaking of himself as if he had always been on the market:

> 'Madame,' quoþ þe myry mon, 'Mary yow ȝelde,
> For I haf founden, in god fayth, yowre fraunchis nobele,
> And oþer ful much of oþer folk fongen bi hor dedez,
> Bot þe daynté þat þay delen, for my disert nys euen,
> Hit is þe worchyp of yourself, þat noȝt bot wel connez.'
>
> (1263–67)

It is unquestionably polite of Gawain to admit so humbly that people are accustomed to pay him more (*daynté . . . delen*) than he deserves (*disert*), but where courtesy ends and commerce begins is in serious doubt here. Gawain is doing his very best to be polite, but he is repeatedly forced to be polite in the Lady's terms, which are commercial terms involving Gawain more and more in the market of relativity. Ever more certainly if also subtly the Lady is convincing Gawain that he has a *price* and that he is marketable. Soon it will be easy to convince him that he is for sale. Indeed, the commercialism of lines 1266–67 is so insistent that it is easy to overlook the less obvious but still incriminating (even if idiomatic and almost formulaic) *Mary yow ȝelde*—'Let Mary repay you for your generosity'—with its barely suppressed implication, "I hope *I* don't have to repay you for all this lush flattery." *ȝelde* as well as other forms of the word (*forȝelde*, for example), though in appearance harmlessly idiomatic, often function in the poem to betray the extent to which commercialism is part of the fabric of feudalism and chivalry. Still more important an indication of Gawain's gradual immersion in commercial relativity is his admission that it is the *worchyp of yourself* in relation to which or measured against which he has any *disert* at all. This is in fact true, but again, it is more courtesy than commerce with Gawain, who does not appreciate the extent to which he is playing into the Lady's hands by according her the privilege of measuring and pricing him.

But that is exactly what he is doing and she wastes no time in seizing the opening he gives her:

> 'Bi Mary,' quoþ þe menskful, 'me þynk hit an oþer;
> For were I *worth* al þe wone of wymmen alyue,
> And al þe *wele* of þe worlde were in my honde,
> And I schulde *chepen* and chose to cheue me a lorde,
> For þe *costes* þat I haf knowen vpon þe, knyȝt, here,

Of bewté and debonerté and blyþe semblaunt,
And þat I haf er herkkened and halde hit here trwee,
Þer schulde no freke vpon folde bifore yow be chosen.'
                              (1268–75; emphasis added)

The Lady is now stepping up the game; the commercial rhetoric is intensifying. With Gawain on display in one of her lord's bedrooms, she has inspected his *cost(es)* and found them *trwee* to their advance billing (*þat I haf er herkkened*); and were she to barter and to dicker (*chepen*) for a mate, she would spare nothing in the world (1269–70) as long as it were hers *in order to buy Gawain*. Knowing the *cost(es)* of Gawain, she would pay, no matter what it might be, the 'cost' of Gawain. In effect, by this point in the seduction, Gawain has been convinced that he 'costs' so much gold, honor, love, what have you; he has been convinced that he has a market *prys* and that he is marketable. And so if he cannot be bought with sex (nor with *wele*; 2037 and 2432), still he can be bought; of this there can no longer be any doubt:

'Iwysse, worþy,' quoþ þe wyȝe, 'ȝe haf waled wel better,
Bot I am proude of þe prys þat ȝe put on me,
And, soberly your seruaunt, my souerayn I holde yow,
And yowre knyȝt I becom, and Kryst yow forȝelde.'
                              (1276–79; emphasis added)

Now the rhetoric of feudalism. Gawain becomes the *seruaunt* of Bertilak's Lady: she becomes his sovereign; he pays her homage (*yowre knyȝt I becom*). And he makes this gesture, an unmistakable act of fealty, because he is proud of the price that she has put on him. Gawain has sold himself already to the Lady, although he does not yet know it; he has alienated to her the right to determine his identity, and she *will* exercise that right. To be sure, Gawain adds, almost as an anxious afterthought, *Kryst yow forȝelde*, but these words should once again give a moment's pause. It is as if Gawain were once more trying to cover himself—saying this time: "Let Christ repay you rather than that I should spend my *cost(es)*." But this anxious afterthought is a bit too late. He has already paid the Lady. The first installment is his pride. If he is proud of the price that she put on him, Gawain is investing his pride in, or paying it to, her estimate of him. And having bought Gawain's pride, Bertilak's Lady has achieved a major success in the *gomen*, which she and her husband are playing for Gawain's benefit.

Gawain's pride, like all pride, is an assertion of personal value to the exclusion of the Maker of that value. Before the extravagant seduction that Bertilak's Lady has enacted, Gawain has gradually—and to his own view, doubtless, imperceptibly—come to assume that he is the maker, the source, of his value. He really is that good, he must assume. Such is the youthful idealist's first step on the way to the radical insistence on private, exclusive value. But when a man assumes that he is his own maker, it becomes painfully easy for another man—or woman—to usurp that role. He or she need only supply what the other person thinks he wants, and the deed is done. Gawain, of course, does want to be *comlokest kyd of his elde*. And the Lady has no trouble in supplying that want, as we have seen. So it is that, become Gawain's maker, she can go on to unmake, as it were, the relationship between Gawain and his name: "'Now he þat spedez vche spech þis disport ʒelde yow! / Bot þat ʒe be Gawan, hit gotz in mynde'" (1292–93). In response to this sly assumption by the Lady of superior authority (she *knows* who Gawain would be), Gawain, exactly as a proud man would, worries first and foremost about formality (cf. Davenport 1978:190): "'Querfore?' quoþ þe freke . . . / Ferde lest he hade fayled *in fourme* of his castes" (1294–95; emphasis added). Which is to miss the point by a very wide margin since he puts courtesy before his soul's health. When Gawain tells Bertilak's Lady, *my souerayn I holde yow*, doubtless he still assumes that he is being merely courteous and mannerly; but oaths—and Gawain of all people should have remembered this—are powerful and have a way of binding a man. And this oath *has* bound Gawain to the Lady, even to the point of jeopardizing his soul. She has become Gawain's maker: she has made his *prys* before his very eyes; and, it appears, she makes his life when she gives him the green girdle that, current for his life, can save it. But so far from saving his life, the green girdle *costs* Gawain his *lewté* and becomes the *syngne of surfet*, where *surfet*, as excess, is a kind of pride. Proud of the price his human maker puts on him, Gawain ultimately pays the price of pride at the Green Chapel and bears the mark of it for the rest of his life.

* * *

Of course, Bertilak's Lady is Gawain's maker only from one perspective and a limited one at that. In a slightly wider perspective, the Green Knight is his maker. He tells Gawain at the Green Chapel, "'I wroʒt hit myseluen'" (2361). But then, he himself is only obeying (so he says) Morgne la Faye's orders. Finally, in the widest perspective, he and Morgne and the Lady, as nature and fortune, are in fact ministers of this sublunary sphere (see chap. 1 at n. 4) directly answerable, presumably, to God. Hence, the Maker himself, presumably, is in control of a *gomen* otherwise potentially infernal and deadly. From the perspective of Gawain's self-image and self-understanding, however, the Lady is his maker. And she exercises her privilege in the third temptation scene. Here she so completely reconstructs Gawain's image in terms of commercial relativity and relationships that he finally believes that value is subjective only and takes thus the making of his life into his own hands.

Gawain's fall into economic reality concludes as the Lady rises from his bed and prepares to leave on the last morning (1796 ff.). That *prynces of pris* who has *depresed him so pikke* (1770) asks him for "'sumquat of þy gifte . . . / Þat I may mynne on þe, mon, my mournyng to lassen'" (1799–1800). Gawain answers again in the commercial rhetoric that has been so insistent in the Lady's discourse: "'Bot to dele yow for drurye þat dawed bot neked'" (1805). Gawain cannot *deal in love* with the Lady because, he says, he has nothing about him on this trip worthy of or equal to what she has deserved (1801–2). She is evidently a *prynces of pris* beyond what Gawain can afford. Indeed, when the poem first introduces her, she is very 'costly':

Ho watz þe fayrest in felle, of flesche and of lyre,
And of compas and colour and *costes*, of alle oþer,
And wener þen Wenore, as þe wyȝe þoȝt.
             (943–45; emphasis added)

Bertilak's Lady is the 'fairest of qualities' (the primary sense of *costes*), but she is also the most *expensive*, as Gawain learns to his chagrin, because her appraisal of his *prys*—her attention to him—costs him his *lewté*. She is a *prynces of pris*, moreover, not only because she is 'costly' but also because she is a shrewd merchant who revels in pricing things.

As, for example, jewels and girdles. If Gawain will not give her a gift, then he will certainly, she says, have a gift of her (1813–16). She offers him a valuable ring *of red golde werkez* (1817). But Gawain refuses the ring because "'I haf none yow to norne, ne noȝt wyl I take'" (1823). This is a crucial moment. Up to this point, Gawain's dealings, both within the larger context of his covenant with Bertilak and within the more restricted context of his *luf-talkyng* with Bertilak's Lady, have been as open and as honest as possible. Although the Lady has exposed Gawain to the commercial relativity inherent in chivalry, Gawain has so far proved a consumer whose consumption is not conspicuous: he has neither committed adultery, to betray his host, nor absolutely scorned the Lady, to abuse her *fin'amors* taste in *luf-talkyng*. But Gawain has, all the same, under the Lady's extraordinary pressure, become a consumer. And it is his consumerism that betrays him now. He refuses the ring, which is a universally acknowledged value, because he has nothing with him with which to pay for it. He accepts, however, the green girdle, which is an obscure and fictive value, because he thinks it is worth his life; and he pays for it with his *lewté*, the most valuable possession in or on his person now or ever.

When Gawain refuses the ring, Bertilak's Lady offers him her girdle, and at first he refuses it too:

> And he nay þat he nolde neghe in no wyse
> Nauþer golde ne garysoun, er God hym grace sende
> To acheue to þe chaunce þat he hade chosen þere.
> 'And þerfore, I pray yow, displese yow noȝt,
> And lettez be your *bisinesse*, for I bayþe hit yow neuer
>   to graunte;
>   I am derely to yow biholde
>   Bicause of your *sembelaunt*,
>   And euer in hot and colde
>   To be your trwe seruant.'
> (1836–45; emphasis added)

Noteworthy here are, first, Gawain's evident awareness of the Lady's *bisinesse*[3]—that she is dickering and dealing—and, second, his insistence on her *sembelaunt*. On the one hand, Gawain knows that the Lady is trying to sell him something—he has learned that much about her during three mornings of temptation—but, on the other hand, he is still bound to appearance—her *sembelaunt*—or to outward shows, forms, graces, what have you, which conceal as much as if not more than they reveal. Gawain is perched, so to speak, on the precarious margin between the real and the apparent or merely fictive, the *sembelaunt*.

The Lady goes on, heedless of his refusal of her girdle:

> 'Now forsake ȝe þis silke,' sayde þe burde þenne,
> 'For hit is symple in hitself? And so hit wel semez.
> Lo! so hit is littel, and lasse hit is *worþy*;

Bot who-so knew þe *costes* þat knit ar þerinne,
He wolde hit *prayse* at more *prys*, parauenture;
For quat gome so is gorde with þis grene lace,
While he hit hade hemely halched aboute,
Þer is no haþel vnder heuen tohewe hym þat myȝt,
For he myȝt not be slayn for slyȝt vpon erþe.'
                    (1846–54; emphasis added)

Although the green girdle is little and seems simple and less worthy
(see 1835), its *cost(es)* by which it is (ap)praised at a high *prys* is(are) no
less than a man's life. The green girdle costs a man's life; that is its
price. Now the only currency that Gawain has in or on his person
equivalent to such *cost(es)* or *prys* is his *lewté*. And so it is that to buy his
life he spends his loyalty.

The crux of Gawain's commercial behavior here is his very refusal
to accept the Lady's gift until she convinces him to take it: which is to
say, until she sells it to him or sells him on it—either modern idiom
will make the point. Note, in this regard, that when Gawain first refuses the ring, the Lady *bede hit hym ful* bysily (1824; emphasis added).
Bysily here, of course, has primarily its Old English denotation of 'ear-
nestly' (T-G-D 1967:169); but the poet brilliantly plays off its commercial connotation to suggest that the Lady *is* trying *to sell* Gawain on
something. And so it is that, in the end, Gawain does not spend his
lewté for a certain reality; rather, he buys a sales pitch, an adver-
tisement. He has no way of knowing whether the Lady is telling him
the truth about the green girdle; he *cannot* know *þe costes þat knit ar
þerinne*. He can only take her word for them; he can only buy her
word. Nothing in the appearance of the girdle suggests its *cost(es)* or
prys. Not even its color, since if the color signaled magic to Gawain, it
would also have to signal the complicity of Bertilak's Lady with the
Green Knight in the plot to behead Gawain. But Gawain receives no
such signal. He simply buys her word paying for it with his *lewté*.

But earlier, he would not accept *a riche rynk of red golde werkez* that
she offered him as a gift (1817). His reason: "'I haf none yow to norne,
ne noȝt wyl I take'" (1823). Gawain has nothing with him on this trip
of equal value to exchange for the ring (1808–10). And yet he exchanges his very definition as a knight—"'my kynde . . . / Þat is larges
and lewté þat longez to knyȝtez'" (2380–81)—for a green girdle that
is a kind of money displacing and representing his life. The value of
gold, of course, is no more inherent than that of lead tokens (or Japa-
nese yen or American dollars);[4] that gold *has* value is glaringly self-
evident, however. Hence the poem's strategy with the ring:

'If ȝe renay my rynk, to ryche for hit semez,
ȝe wolde not so hyȝly halden be to me,
I schal gif yow my girdel, þat gaynes yow lasse.'
(1827–29)

The ring *seems* too rich. The poem lavishes four lines on the description of the ring (1817–20) for the very purpose of insisting on its universally acknowledged value—"Wyt ȝe wel, hit watz worth wele ful hoge" (1820)—which Gawain is rejecting for a value apparent only to him—namely, the green girdle. It is thus that the poem can expose the extent to which subjectivity has vitiated Gawain's reasoning. From a young and idealistic conviction of the inherent value of things to a private certainty that all value is only subjective, Gawain has moved so recklessly that he has, in effect, abandoned reason. Because the ring seems too rich—so that Gawain would *hyȝly halden be* to the Lady for it—he refuses it. *But* he turns around and accepts the girdle, a piece of cloth tricked out in gold (1832, 2038–39, 2395), precisely because it *seems to him* as rich as his own life, for which, in turn, he becomes *hyȝly halden* to the Lady. The universally acknowledged value, which *seems* too rich to Gawain, is therefore much cheaper than the merely apparent value, which can *only* seem rich *and* only to Gawain. Clearly, fiction has supplanted reality. Nor does the irony in the Lady's offer of the girdle stop here. The girdle does not *gayne* Gawain less; it appears to gain him his life. And yet, it does *gayne* Gawain less because it costs him his *lewté*. These vertiginous subversions of reality and meaning are themselves signs of the erosion of reason that sets in when the relativity of value leads to unrestrained subjectivity. By means of her high-pressure *bisinesse* tactics, the Lady has succeeded in seducing Gawain into believing that value lies only in the subjectivity that prices it. By convincing Gawain that she is a very good judge of knight's flesh, she also convinced him that she is to be trusted in all her pricings, including that of the green girdle. Since, moreover, she had become his maker, in a sense ('*my souerayn I holde yow*,' he told her) Gawain is especially vulnerable to identifying his subjectivity with hers. Hence the text's earlier empahsis on his awareness of her *bisinesse* while he still insists on honoring her *sembelaunce* (1840 and 1843): he knows he is in peril but he is also fascinated with the agent of his peril. Gawain is ripe for giving up his identity to Bertilak's Lady. So it is that when she praises/prices the green girdle—when she lavishes words on it—Gawain buys/consumes her words because they have effectively become *his own*. And in the process he begins to obscure reality with language since

> hit come to his hert
> Hit [the girdle] were a *juel* for þe jopardé þat hym iugged were.
>   (1855–56; emphasis added)

The actual jewel, the *riche rynk of red golde werkez*, Gawain rejects; instead, he accepts a jewel that can only be a jewel by his exclusively private evaluation of it as such. Bewitched by Bertilak's Lady, Gawain's error is the error of reducing the world to his own view of the world. As such, it is also the error of assuming that he is complete and sufficient to determine the meaning of his life. It is, finally, the error of idolatry. And this, he eventually perceives, is a grave error indeed.

iii. The Law and Its Limits

To [wynne] *hym to woȝe* (1550), where the verb *wynne/wonnen* obliquely but surely suggests her commercial strategy, Bertilak's Lady manipulates Gawain until he insists on private value exclusively. She convinces Gawain that everything has its price, including his life and *lewté*, and in doing so, she reduces him to a consumer. In all this she resembles certain other women whom the poem mentions:

> 'Bot hit is no ferly þaȝ a fole madde,
> And þurȝ wyles of wymmen be *wonen* to sorȝe,
> For so watz Adam in erde with one bygyled,
> And Salamon with fele sere, and Samson eftsonez—
> Dalyda dalt hym hys wyrde—and Dauyth þerafter
> Watz blended with Barsabe, þat much bale þoled.
> Now þese were wrathed wyth her wyles, hit were a *wynne* huge
> To luf hom wel, and leue hem not, a leude þat couþe.
> For þes wer forne þe freest, þat folȝed alle þe sele
> Exellently of alle þyse oþer, vnder heuenryche
>   þat mused.'
>   (2414–24; emphasis added)

Others have remarked the unexpected vehemence of this interlude of typical medieval misogyny (e.g., Burrow 1965: 147–48; Spearing 1970:220; 223–24). And I am no surer than they why its tone is so vehement. But I would suggest that part of the motive for the passage is Gawain's use of commercial discourse—*wonen* and *wynne*—to communicate his feelings. This is not the first time, of course, that he has used such discourse. But it is the first time that he uses it in such a way as to demonstrate that he understands the importance of relativity and relationships to his own condition. He, like all these others, was won to sorrow, and he now understands how 'profitable' (*wynne huge*) it would be to love women without trusting them. Though his misogyny may be distasteful, Gawain's awareness of the commerce of human affairs is vastly improved. Gawain knows now that people do not exist as isolated integers of pure value but as complicated entities in a web of relations largely commercial and therefore liable to sudden fluctuation. He knows now that people can be bought and sold and can buy and sell and still be very good people or, at least, very human. He has, in short, grown up a little in the *sorȝe* to which the Lady won him.

But she was not alone in working this change in Gawain. Joining her in the *assay* (2362 as well as 2457) of Gawain's *surquidré* is Bertilak. He completes the *gomen* that exposes Gawain to relativity and relationship by maneuvering him constantly into merchandising—into becoming a merchant. Forced into consumerism, on the one hand, and into merchandising, on the other, Gawain is so immersed in commercial reality that he can finally experience, at the Green Chapel, that he is, like all men—Adam included—incomplete and therefore in need of relation. Despite wounded pride, misogyny, and the fitful desire to justify himself, Gawain learns—he is, after all, a good man— that no one is an isolated integer of pure value.

Until his test has transpired, however, Gawain misunderstands the commerce of human affairs, and therefore he fails to appreciate the necessity of relativity and relationships in the generation of values. Crucial to an explanation of his misunderstanding and of his failure is the poem's emphasis on covenants and legality. It is principally by means of covenants that Bertilak succeeds in forcing Gawain into merchandising; therefore, we need to survey now the role of covenants in the poem.

Of the many other commercial words in the poem after *prys* and *cost(es)*, *couenaunt* is arguably the most pervasive in its influence.[5] In the first place, the *couenaunt* between Gawain and the Green Knight envelops the whole action of the poem and is always more or less in the reader's field of vision. This idea dominates, in part, because the word enjoys commercial and sacred connotations equally. This balance is properly in keeping with the Hebrew word of the Old Testament which it translates: *berith* (OED C:1101) means 'contract' or 'bargain' and refers to the agreements between Jahweh and his chosen people. There is obviously something commercial about those agreements since there are numerous stipulated exchanges between Jahweh and his people. But there is no sharp line between the commercial and the sacred: debts can be of love or of money (tithes, for example) and often of both; and I do not think that a sharp line should be introduced between the commercial and the sacred or between them and any other feature in the *couenaunts* of *Sir Gawain*, either. Though kisses are trivial wares (1945–47, for example), there is something undoubtedly commercial *and* sacred about a man's head: it can be numbered for buying and for sacrificing. The definition of *couenaunt* then should not be so rigorous as to falsify its scope. Gawain and the Green Knight enter into a *couenaunt* at once commercial and sacred: it involves the most material sorts of things—kisses and carcasses—and the most immaterial, too—a man's *lewté* and *trawþe*.

In addition to commercial and sacred connotations, the word *couenaunt* also possessed an explicit legal meaning in the later Middle Ages. Medieval English law recognized a writ of covenant which I pause to mention because of its technical Latin formulas, *breve de conventione* and *placitum conventionis* (Pollock and Maitland 1968:2, 216–17). The word *couenaunt* like 'convention' derives from the Latin *convenio, -ire*; and the legal formulas demonstrate that the 'conventionality' of *couenaunts* was a live property of the word in later Middle English.[6] This association is of importance to *Sir Gawain* because of the poem's obvious concern with the uses and, one might say, the morality of conventionality. Signs, of course, are conventional, as are poems themselves. And if Gawain and the Green Knight establish a *couenaunt* between them, they also establish—though indirectly and latterly—a new convention for Arthur's court: the green girdle as the badge of Arthur's retainers. Making covenants and making signs are crucially related in *Sir Gawain*: values—linguistic, commercial, moral, and spiritual—are a function of convention, itself a force of human community and concert, and as such they depend on the vision and the power and the goodness of the community. To *assay þe surquidré* of Arthur's court is to *assay* its right to the making of conventions and hence values, too. Only after Gawain undergoes the equivalent of the fundamentally mediatory and significatory rite of circumcision can he return to Arthur's court and make a new convention; only after Gawain and through him the *surquidré* of Arthur's court are humbled can a new covenant be made.

In a Christian context, the word *couenaunt* can hardly fail to evoke the two covenants of the Old and the New Dispensations. The poet, I think, relied on this evocation. At line 844, the poem reports that Bertilak is of *hyghe eldee*; the T-G-D edition glosses this phrase, rightly in my opinion, as meaning 'the prime of life'. Very perplexing, therefore, is the description of Bertilak, at the end of the second fitt, just after he and Gawain have agreed to the exchange of winnings:

To bed ȝet er þay ȝede,
Recorded couenauntez ofte;
Þe *olde* lorde of þat leude
Cowþe wel halde layk alofte.
                    (1122–25; emphasis added)

If Bertilak is in 'the prime of life' he can hardly be old in the sense of that word that initially occurs to us. *Olde*, therefore, would seem to have other than its literal meaning. I believe that the word—coming as it does just after Gawain and Bertilak have concluded another *bargayn* (1112) and after they have been rehearsing its terms (*couenauntez*)—serves to suggest Bertilak's (and thus the Green Knight's) Old Testament figural dimensions. The Green Knight administers circumcision to Gawain; he is a figure of nature shrouded in magic; as Bertilak he is the old lord of his people—all these characteristics suggest the Old Law. Hence, while Bertilak (the Green Knight) is also, unquestionably, a Christian figure under the New Dispensation, the poem still expresses in him something of the Old Dispensation. And this above all because he is a maker of laws, rules, bargains, games, rituals, and so forth. Bertilak (the Green Knight) is a figure of the Law that is a property of the Old Dispensation. I am not claiming that Bertilak is first an Old Testament figure and therefore involved with the Law; rather, I am claiming that he is involved with the Law and therefore has figural dimensions of the Old Testament. Similarly, *Sir Gawain* is not an Old Testament poem and therefore legalistic; rather, *Sir Gawain* is concerned with the Law and is thus dependent, to a certain extent, on the Old Testament.[7]

The Old Testament is the Old Law. From the Christian perspective, the most glaring feature of the Old Law is its incompleteness. "'Do not think that I have come to destroy the Law or the Prophets. I have not come to destroy, but to fulfill'" (Matt. 5. 17). The Old Law is incomplete because, as St. Paul discovered in his own person, the Jewish people, though given the Law as Jahweh's chosen and thus superior to all other people, still could not achieve each his own justification—could not generate his own righteousness. In possession of the Law, then, which demanded perfection and programmed its achievement, he still could not become perfect. Rather, in the throes of such a contradiction, his heart became hard even as the Tables of Stone, and he died by the Law (see Rom. 7. 7–24). To demand of the flesh that it become the Law—so completely true to the Law that it is identical to the Law—is to demand that the flesh die. But nothing in the Old Law, as St. Paul suddenly perceived on the road to Damascus, enables the flesh to fulfill let alone endure this awful demand. The flesh wants to live—"Bot for ȝe lufed your lyf; þe lasse I yow blame"—and man cannot eliminate that residue of desire. Only God can. Hence the Mediator, the Verbum, became flesh in order that the flesh might become the Word. Without the Mediator, flesh is condemned to desire completion it can never achieve. Without the Mediator, flesh can know the Law but never obey it. Gawain knows the Law, and he is always careful to observe its rituals (see 753–58, for example); moreover, with the Green Knight he makes laws—covenants, bargains, rules, games. But Gawain is not yet humble, does not yet fathom the meaning of the rituals he observes. He does not appreciate *þe faut and þe fayntyse of þe flesche crabbed*: he must, as he does, learn its *prys—how tender hit is to entyse teches of fylþe*. Without this appreciation he cannot understand the rituals for what they are: nourishment for and support of the *fayntyse* of the flesh. As a knight whose *kynde / . . .* [is] *larges and lewté* Gawain is always involved with Law; but as a man, a creature of flesh, Gawain can never be perfectly loyal to any law—he is too weak. So it is that the poem *Sir Gawain* is concerned with the Law; so it is that it depends on the fundamental lesson of the Old Testament. And, finally, such precision on the point of the Law is the foundation of the poem's Christian significance.

* * *

Gawain and Bertilak (the Green Knight) enter into two *couenaunts* in the poem: one, the more embracing though not necessarily the more important one, is the beheading agreement; the other, slighter and less dramatic though not a jot less important, is the exchange of winnings agreement at Hautdesert. Gawain's failure in the latter *couenaunt* is intelligible as a moral letdown after the strenuous effort of honoring the former. Because he has kept the terms of an agreement that to all appearances must cost him his life, Gawain is all the more prone to rationalize the tiny slip of retaining a wisp of cloth which he owes to his host. Because his *trawþe* is so great in the one case, it shows a slight (quite human) chink in the other.

When the Green Knight bursts upon Arthur's Christmas feast, he proposes his *gomen* (273), the first of the two *couenaunts*, in very legalistic terms, even to *quit-claymyng* his ax (293). Just how legalistic his terms are may possibly be measurable by the role of the *festucca* in medieval English contract law (Pollock and Maitland 1968:2, 187; emphasis added):

In later times "the rod" plays a part in the conveyance of land, and is perhaps still more often used when there is a "quit-claim," a renunciation of rights; but we sometimes hear of it also when "faith" is "made." Hengham tells us that when an essoiner promises that his principal will appear and warrant the essoin, he makes his faith upon the crier's wand, and we find the free miner of the Forest of Dean making his faith *upon a holly stick*.

The cases are not the same, of course: the free miner is swearing that a debt is owed to him; the Green Knight is rather proposing a *gomen* which will result in a debt owed to him. Nevertheless, there is enough similarity to see in the Green Knight's stick of holly (*holyn bobbe*, 206) not only a symbol of peace but also a symbol of formal contract. Moreover, the use that Pollock and Maitland mention of the rod, or *festucca*, in actions of "quit-claim" is possibly quite pertinent. Elsewhere (1968:2, 91, and 187) they note that

> the curious term *quietum clamare* . . . is extremely common, especially when the right that is to be transferred is an adverse right; for example, a disseisee will quit-claim his disseisor [that is, one who owes something, as the Green Knight owes his ax to whoever beheads him, "quits" all "claims" which he might have on the object]. Very possibly in the past such transactions have been effected without written instruments. We often read of the transfer of a rod in connexion with a quit-claim, and the term itself may point to some formal renunciatory cry.

Hence, the Green Knight may bear the stick of holly as, doubtless among other things, a legal token of his faith in the contract he proposes to make.

Be that as it may, there is no denying his legalism, just as there is no denying Gawain's equally legalistic response:

> 'In god fayth . . . Gawan I hatte,
> Þat bede þe þis buffet, quat-so bifallez after,
> And at þis tyme twelmonyth take at þe an oþer
> Wyth what weppen so þou wylt, and wyth no wyȝ ellez
>   on lyue.'   (381–85)

The Green Knight acknowledges Gawain's legal formality and goes on to emphasize the economics of the contract:

'And þou hatz redily rehersed, bi resoun ful trwe,
Clanly al þe couenaunt þat I þe kynge asked,
Saf þat þou schal siker me, segge, bi þi trawþe,
Þat þou schal seche me þiself, wher-so þou hopes
I may be funde vpon folde, and foch þe *such wages*
As þou *deles* me to-day bifore þis douþe ryche.'
                              (392–97; emphasis added)

Gawain will go to the Green Chapel to fetch his *wages*; and there indeed the Green Knight will *pay* him his *wages*: "'Haf þy helme of þy
hede, and haf here þy *pay*'" (2247; emphasis added; cf. 2341). The
terms of the contract are exact; the law is ironclad, so much so that
when Gawain cannot take any more, the Green Knight continues his
legalistic precision with a formal release (*relaxatio*; Pollock and Maitland 1968:2, 91): "'I relece þe of þe remnaunt of ryȝtes alle oþer'"
(2342). When Gawain cannot fulfill the law, he is legally released from
his obligation.

Now this formal release deserves closer scrutiny. Gawain and the
Green Knight obviously engage in a business transaction at the Green
Chapel: "'If any wyȝe oȝt wyl, wynne hider fast, / Oþer now oþer
neuer, *his nedez to spede*'" (2215–16; emphasis added), exclaims Gawain
when he first arrives at the chapel. In this transaction, the text is unambiguous, Gawain is to receive wages and the Green Knight is to pay
him. Not only the earlier passage recounting the Green Knight's terms
to Gawain in Arthur's court but also two others make this very clear:

'To þe grene chapel þou chose, I charge þe, to fotte
Such a dunt as þou hatz dalt—disserued þou habbez
To be ȝederly *ȝolden* on Nw ȝeres morn.'
                              (451–53; emphasis added)

'And þou knowez þe couenauntez kest vus bytwene:
At þis tyme twelmonyth þou toke þat þe falled,
And I schulde at þis Nwe ȝere ȝeply þe *quyte*.'
                              (2242–44; emphasis added)

At the same time, the text is, as we have seen, equally unambiguous
that Gawain owes the Green Knight a debt from which he is released.
Hence Gawain is receiving wages when he is paying a debt. Gawain's
wages are paradoxically his debt. The Green Knight pays Gawain
(though only partially, with a nick in the neck) what Gawain owes him

and cannot pay in full (decapitation). The text, therefore, suggests wages that are a debt, a reward that is a liability, a gain that is a loss.

Behind this suggestion, I think, lies the authority of St. Paul: "Stipendia enim peccati, mors (For the wages of sin are death)" (Rom. 6.23). The wages of sin, or death, are a debt owed to nature. For he who sins and is not redeemed uses his flesh, which is nature's, to his own selfish pleasures, but nature eventually collects its own at death when it reclaims the flesh just as the devil collects his own when he claims the sinful soul (the devil, of course, cannot reclaim the soul).[8] Because of his refusal to accept mortality (*nostram humanitatem*), Gawain has reaped the wages of sin, or death, that he owes to the Green Knight, who is, on one level, the figure of nature. Because Gawain is too proud to lay his life down, as every man must, he has to face the alternative of having his life forcibly taken from him. However, the Green Knight, if a figure of nature, is not, to Gawain's lasting spiritual health, nature *sub lege*.[9] Nature *sub lege* can only kill in the merciless surge of generation and corruption (this surge is brilliantly suggested by the poem in lines 498–99: "A ȝere ȝernes ful ȝerne, and ȝeldez neuer lyke, / Þe forme to þe fynisment foldez ful selden"). The Green Knight, on the contrary, is nature *sub gratia*, which can interrupt the surge of generation and corruption through the power of the Mediator who redeemed fallen nature, and can release a man from the wages of sin, *þe remnaunt of ryȝtes alle oþer*. Nature *sub gratia*, which, in the human frame of reference, we understand to be man in his flesh redeemed, can repent, can suffer as penance, and thus lay life down in that affirmation that raises life up; and the figure of nature *sub gratia*, such as the Green Knight, can confess or administer the sacrament of penance. There is always in nature the possibility of change (thus the poem's repeated emphasis on the seasons); and in nature redeemed, such change can be more than mere mutability, it can be conversion. Even death can die (Hos. 13. 14 and 1 Cor. 15. 55).

Hence the Green Knight does not pay Gawain his full wages, for which Gawain is indebted to him: he does not decapitate him; he only nicks him in the neck. Whereupon, he not only releases Gawain from the remainder of the debt (*ryȝtez*); he also absolves him of his sin—"'I halde þe polysed of þat plyȝt, and pured as clene, / As þou hadez neuer forfeted syþen þou watz fyrst borne.'" The Green Knight, therefore, is of the Old Testament in that he makes laws, covenants, contracts, and rules by which he tests Gawain; he is of the Old Testament also in that he administers circumcision, the *sacramentum Mediatoris*, to Gawain. But he is also of the New Testament in that he has the authority to confess, to exact penance from, and to absolve Gawain of his sin. He is of the Old Testament insofar as he must teach Gawain the weight of the Law in the flesh; he is of the New Testament insofar as he thereupon lifts that weight as far as it can be lifted in this life. The wages of sin are death, but they do not have to be collected, that is, paid. When Gawain reports to Arthur's court his adventure, he *þe lace hondeled* and lamented that "'þis is þe laþe and þe *losse* þat I laȝt haue / Of couardise and couetyse þat I haf caȝt þare'" (2505–8; emphasis added). The green girdle is a *loss*—as it were, damages. But it could have been worse. Gawain could have had to pay, that is, collect the wages of sin.

The Green Knight releases Gawain from the *remnaunts of ryȝtes alle oþer* because Gawain literally cannot collect his wages, pay his debt: "'þaȝ my hede falle on þe stonez, / I con not hit restore'" (2282–83). Because Gawain cannot re-attach his head, he flinches at the Green Knight's first blow. But although this is a failure—and the Green Knight does capitalize on it (2270–79)—it is not Gawain's most serious failure nor the one, finally, because of which he is circumcised at the Green Chapel. The Green Knight explains at length:

'Fyrst I mansed þe muryly with a mynt one,
And roue þe wyth no rof-sore, with ryȝt I þe profered
For þe forwarde þat we fest in þe fyrst nyȝt,
And þou trystyly þe trawþe and trwly me haldez,
Al þe gayne þow me gef, as god mon schulde.
Þat oþer munt for þe morne, mon, I þe profered,
Þou kyssedes my clere wyf—þe cossez me raȝtez.
For boþe two here I þe bede bot two bare myntes
          boute scaþe.
    Trwe mon trwe restore,
    Þenne þaṫ mon drede no waþe.
    At þe þrid þou fayled þore,
    And þerfor þat tappe ta þe.'
                                        (2345–57)

Gawain takes the *tappe* because he did not *restore* the green girdle to Bertilak. The phrase *Trwe mon trwe restore* defies translation because modern English is impoverished of the ethical *vis*[10] compressed in these Middle English words. A rough and ready paraphrase is probably the best that can be expected: something like 'the one who is true the way truth itself is true must restore with an equal truth'. But

Gawain cannot be true as a universal is true, for, as a man, he is immersed in, bound to, time: '*At þe þrid þou fayled þore.*' As important as the verb 'failed' is the noun 'third', for it marks Gawain's temporality—which is to say, his humanity. Once, perhaps twice, Gawain approaches the absolute ideal of *Trwe mon trwe restore*, but risk increases with frequency, and if *þrid tyme þrowe best* (1680)—where the mysterious fullness of the number three would somehow confirm Gawain's ideality and universality—the third time, alas, proves one time too many for Gawain's mortal endurance. He cannot live up to (or into) the ideal three times in a row because time, which is mortality, claims him as its creature. Gawain, because he is human, cannot escape time any more than he can fulfill the law; he cannot live without relationships nor apart from relativity. This is the limit of the Law: Gawain cannot be *trwe*.

iv. From Price to Pricing

Gawain fails to be *trwe* because he does not honor his covenant or agreement with Bertilak to exchange winnings. He becomes finally too compulsive a merchant to maintain such honor and this because he is too selfish a consumer. Because he covets his life, he dickers and deals with Bertilak, always holding something back, until finally he lies to him, having concealed the green girdle. But when he sets out from Arthur's court, Gawain is far from being a compulsive merchant—or even a merchant at all. In fact, he is virtually innocent of merchandising, and this is his fundamental dilemma.

His problematic innocence is first clearly visible when he asks Arthur leave to seek the Green Chapel:

> 'Now, lege lorde of my lyf, leue I yow ask;
> 3e knowe *þe cost of þis cace*, kepe I no more
> To telle yow tenez þerof, neuer bot trifel;
> Bot I am boun to þe bur barely to-morne
> To sech þe gome of þe grene, as God wyl me wysse.'
> (545–49; emphasis added)

It would demean the poem not to hear the homonym in the 'cost of this case': in a sense, neither Gawain, despite what he says, nor Arthur yet knows the *cost* because each, in the *surquidré* of his youthful idealism, fails to appreciate the import of the Green Knight's *gomen*, not to mention the significance of *cost* itself. A similar conclusion arises from Gawain's anxiety, later, over observing Christmas mass:

Þe gome vpon Gryngolet glydez hem vnder,
Þur3 mony misy and myre, mon al hym one,
Carande for his costes, lest he ne keuer schulde
To se þe seruyse of þat syre, þat on þat self ny3t
Of a burde watz borne *oure baret to quelle*.
(748–52; emphasis added)

If Gawain is "anxious about his obligations," he is also concerned with
formality yet again. It is not a question here of sincerity or insincerity.
Gawain is undoubtedly sincere. It is a question rather of understanding. Does he really understand *his costes*? The text suggests an answer
to this question. Christ was born, this passage tells us, *oure baret to
quelle* (752). Now almost the first thing we learn in the poem about
Arthur's and Gawain's ancestors is that they were *bolde . . . baret þat
lofden* (21). And like father, like son: certainly Arthur's and Gawain's
behavior at the earlier Christmas feast suggests that they *love strife*, especially since Arthur will not eat until *hym deuised were*

Of sum auenturus þyng an vncouþe tale,
Of sum mayn meruayle, þat he my3t trawe,
Of alderes, of armes, of oþer auenturus,
Oþer sum segg hym biso3t of sum siker kny3t
To joyne wyth hym in iustyng, in jopardé to lay,
Lede, lif for lyf, leue vchon oþer,
As fortune wolde fulsun hom, þe fayrer to haue.
(93–99)

Such an attitude—of loving *baret*—at the feast of one born *to quelle
baret* argues ignorance of, or, at the very least insensitivity to, the
meaning of that feast and of the event it celebrates. Nor is Gawain innocent of this ignorance or insensitivity: he enjoyed hefting that ax,
we can be sure. Hence his "anxiety about his obligations" sits ill with
his actual behavior, and this inconsistency suggests that he does not
really understand *his costes* and the relationships they entail. It is for
this reason that Bertilak's Lady and indeed Bertilak's whole household enmesh Gawain in the market of human affairs immediately
upon his arrival at Hautdesert. In a sense, it is their duty to chasten
Gawain's *surquidré* by demonstrating to him how incomplete he is, how
very far he is from understanding his obligations.

Because he does not and cannot yet really know the *cost(es)* of
things, Gawain is quite ready, once at Hautdesert, to make a bargain
with his host:

'ȝet firre,' quoþ þe freke, 'a forwarde we make:
Quat-so-euer I wynne in þe wod hit worþez to yourez,
And quat *chek* so ȝe acheue *chaunge* me þerforne.
Swete, swap we so, sware with trawþe,
Queþer, leude, so lymp, lere oþer better.'
'Bi God,' quoþ Gawayn þe gode, 'I grant þertylle,
And þat yow lyst for to layke, lef hit me þynkes.'
'Who bryngez vus þis beuerage, þis *bargayn* is maked.'
                    (1105–12; emphasis added)

Significant here is Gawain's commitment of himself to fortune: *chek*
and *chaunge* locate the very caprice and instability of the fickle lady
who rules this sublunary sphere.[11] A later passage of the third fitt further confirms Gawain's surrender to fortune:

And efte in her bourdyng þay bayþen in þe morn
To fylle þe same forwardez þat þay byfore maden:
Wat chaunce so bytydez hor cheuysaunce to chaunge,
What nwez so þay nome, at naȝt quen þay metten.
                    (1404–7; emphasis added)

Gawain agrees, then, if not to a game of chance, to a game at least
contingent on chance; and Bertilak's Lady, who figures one of the
faces of fortune, wastes little time in starting the play. Having re-
signed himself to *chek* and *chaunge*, not really knowing the cost of his
case, Gawain must see it through until the end when he will be himself
checked and changed.

At the end of the first hunt, Bertilak prepares to exchange his winnings with Gawain. He asks him, as part of his effort to further the
gomen of humbling him: "'Haf I prys wonnen?'" (1379). Gawain's reply betrays the merchant in him:

'ȝe iwysse,' quoþ þat oþer wyȝe, 'here is wayth fayrest
Þat I seȝ þis seuen ȝere in sesoun of wynter.'
'And al I gif yow, Gawayn,' quoþ þe gome þenne,
'For by acorde of couenaunt ȝe craue hit as your awen.'
'Þis is soth,' quoþ þe segge, 'I say yow þat ilke:
Þat I haf worthyly wonnen þis wonez wythinne,
Iwysse with as god wylle hit worþez to ȝourez.'
                    (1381–87)

From here he proceeds to kiss Bertilak, saying, just as a merchant

would, "'Tas yow þere my cheuicaunce, I cheued no more'" (1390).
But Bertilak is not content with this. He begins even now to press his
advantage:

> 'Hit is god,' quoþ þe godmon, 'grant mercy þerfore.
> Hit may be such hit is þe better, and 3e me breue wolde
> Where 3e wan þis ilk wele bi wytte of yorseluen.'
> (1392–94)

But Gawain is opportunistic—he learns very fast, though he learns
more by rote than with real understanding. In fact, quite formula-
ically, he retreats immediately into the letter of the law:

> 'Þat watz not *forward*,' quoþ he, 'frayst me no more.
> For 3e haf tan þat yow *tydez*, trawe non oþer
>   3e mowe.'   (1395–97; emphasis added)

The formalities and the rhetoric of merchandising and contractual
agreements begin to dominate Gawain's relations with the household
at Hautdesert. As far as he is concerned or knows, he is only playing a
game. He will soon realize, however, not only that the game has very
high stakes indeed but also that it *has* stakes. The game is a wager
which stakes relative goods one against the other; it therefore assumes
that some goods are better than others. So far in his life this axiom has
touched Gawain only as a formality. Things are about to change,
however, as he experiences more and more of the economics of his
situation.

At the end of the second hunt, Gawain again prices Bertilak's catch
(1630) and goes on to bestow upon him yet more kisses:

> 'Now ar we euen,' quoþ þe haþel, 'in þis euentide
> Of alle þe couenauntes þat we knyt, syþen I com hider,
>   bi lawe.'
>   Þe lorde sayde, 'Bi saynt Gile,
>   3e ar þe best þat I knowe!
>   3e ben ryche in a whyle,
>   Such chaffer and 3e drowe.'   (1641–47)

Here insistent legal terminology supplements Gawain's commercial
rhetoric. As if to keep one step ahead of his unwitting pupil, Bertilak,
in response, intensifies the commercial rhetoric, referring to his and
Gawain's exchange as a *chaffer* or trade. Such insistence on the com-

merce of human affairs must wear Gawain down. Indeed, Bertilak and his Lady do not miss a chance to lead Gawain deeper into such commerce. For example, during the evening after the second hunt, Bertilak's Lady reduces Gawain to some rather uncomfortable merchandising:

> And euer oure luflych kny3t [was] þe lady bisyde.
> Such semblaunt to þat segge semly ho made
> Wyth stille stollen countenaunce, þat stalworth to plese,
> Þat al forwondered watz þe wy3e, and wroth with hymseluen,
> *Bot he nolde not for his nurture nurne hir a3aynez,*
> *Bot dalt with hir al in daynté,* how-se-euer þe dede turned
>   towrast.   (1657−63; emphasis added)

Although a gentleman (*for his nurture*) who does not spurn ladies, Gawain is also a merchant who deals *in daynté* with them, and this even though they are thieves (*wyth stille* stollen *countenaunce*). If his discomfort is owing to his *nurture*, still Gawain's recourse from that discomfort is commercial, a 'dealing in courtesy', no matter how the deed and its outcome trouble him (*turned towrast*); and such recourse demonstrates, indeed even insists, that his gentlemanliness or *nurture* cannot avoid commerce. Gawain is made even more aware of the dependence of his *nurture* on commerce immediately after his dealing with the Lady. He turns, doubtless with some sense of relief, to his host and *craue[s] leue to kayre on þe morn,*

> For hit watz ne3 at þe terme þat he to schulde.
> Þe lorde hym letted of þat, to lenge hym resteyed,
> And sayde, 'As I am trwe segge, I siker my trawþe
> Þou schal cheue to þe grene chapel þy *charres* to make.'
>   (1670−74; emphasis added)

Bertilak's choice of words for Gawain's imminent confrontation, or *charres* ('business'), can only thrust upon the knight once more how deeply involved in commerce his knightly duties and thus his *nurture* are.

The collaborators at Hautdesert quicken the tempo of the *gomen* at the end of the third hunt, when Bertilak returns with the pelt of the fox, who is called a *þef* (1725). At this point in the *gomen* Gawain sinks so far into consumerism and merchandising that he comes to resemble the archetypal shady dealer or a common, conniving, double-dealing thief.[12] Harsh words, many will object, but justified. This time it is

Gawain who approaches Bertilak *first* to make the exchange—such eagerness can hardly fail to suggest to us some guilt at having accepted and concealed the girdle (Burrow 1965:111)—and, furthermore, he is most prim and punctilious in his legal formality as he makes the exchange:

> 'I schal fylle vpon fyrst oure forwardez nouþe,
> Þat we spedly han spoken, þer spared watz no drynk.'
>   (1934–35)

Bertilak, of course, is well aware of what is afoot and loses no time in trapping Gawain in a shady deal even as he earlier this same day had trapped that other thief, the fox:

> 'Bi Kryst,' quoþ þat oþer kny3t, '3e cach much sele
> In cheuisaunce of þis chaffer, 3if 3e hade goud chepez.'
>   (1938–39)

The lines imply a question ("*if* you had good terms?") and a leading question if ever there was one. *Sele,* or 'happiness', also means 'fortune' (AS *sæl*) and all three alliterating words in line 1939 are commercial. A paraphrase of Bertilak's assertion (which is also a question) might read: "If you had good terms (?), you catch much happiness in the dickering for and winning of this merchandise." Between the lines, as it were, Bertilak is implying, "if you are as shrewd a merchant (*3if 3e hade goud chepez*) as these wares suggest (*in cheuisaunce of þis chaffer*), you are snug in the lap of fortune (*3e cach much sele*)." And Gawain confirms his guilt by dodging the leading question to tell a lie rather than the *trawþe* that Bertilak would expect from a *perfect* knight. Rather than something like, "Yes, I have become rather the merchant, you know, all tangled up in this trading business, and I must say, it leaves me a bit uncomfortable, uncertain of myself," Gawain insists, damningly:

> '3e, of þe chepe no charg,' . . .
> 'As is pertly payed þe chepez þat I a3te.'
>   (1940–41)

Gawain, hardly innocent any longer (and this, of course, is why the fox is hunted last), urges upon Bertilak his, Gawain's, very own mistake: "Pay the cost (*chepe*) no mind, ignore the terms, because I have paid you the goods I owe you." Gawain has precisely ignored the cost of the green girdle and compounds his ignorance with a lie, in the telling of which he finalizes the sale of his *lewté* and *trawþe*. A merchant indeed is this knight *comlokest kyd of his elde*. Just such a merchant as was Adam in that "first prevarication," that primal lie, because of which "the covenant of life entrusted to man in Paradise" was broken (see chap. 2 at n. 6).

Bertilak responds with the irony that Gawain's lie deserves (and the irony just possibly stings Gawain):

> 'Mary,' quoþ þat oþer mon, 'myn is bihynde,
> For I haf hunted al þis day, and noȝt haf I geten
> Bot þis foule fox felle—þe fende haf þe godez!—
> And þat is ful pore for to pay for suche *prys þinges*
> As ȝe haf þryȝt me here þro, suche þre cosses
>   so gode.'   (1942–47; emphasis added)

If poor pay for the *prys* kisses that Gawain has bestowed upon him, Bertilak's *foule fox felle*, the devil's own merchandise (1944), is more than appropriate pay for Gawain's treachery—the hide of a thief to reward a thief. And then—very damning—"'Inoȝ,' quoþ Sir Gawayn, / 'I þonk yow, bi þe rode'" (1948–49; emphasis added). The abrupt, almost curt reply, *Inoȝ*, betrays the traitor—who is *Sir* Gawain, as the text takes pains to remind us at just this moment—and his pangs of guilt.

From the predicament in which he now finds himself, Gawain can be redeemed only by powers greater than man's. Gawain has lied and kept what is not his. So enmeshed in commerce now that he has insisted on private value to the exclusion of all relations, Gawain has succumbed to a pride the obverse of that which skews Arthur's court and plagues even his best knight. There, in *surquidré*, as knight of the pentangle and of the Virgin Mary, Gawain presumed and presumed *upon* relation and relationships without giving thought to the humanity and consequent fallibility of either:

> 'Bot for as much as ȝe ar myn em I am only *to prayse*,
> No *bounté* bot your blod I in my bodé knowe.'
>   (356–57; emphasis added)

Here are economics and commercial language, to be sure, no doubt of that, expressing relation and even blood relationships; and they continue, though with a different emphasis, in the next line (358) with *note*. But it is all formality—fastidious politeness—answering to the

sheer formality of Arthur's leaping to accept the Green Knight's challenge without giving a thought to the implications of the challenge
(Benson 1965:214–15). Indeed, the whole speech from which these
lines are taken (343–61) is a study in the overripeness of *cortaysye*
where convoluted, ingenious syntax expresses material relations that
are presumptions at best, downright vanity at worst. A. C. Spearing's
(1972:43–50) remains the best analysis of the syntax of Gawain's first
speech. His analysis shows that this syntax is a kind of overrefined,
overbred nervousness: "The sense one has in moving through the
passage is of the skirting of obstacles, the overcoming or evading of
one difficulty after another: the syntax seems to wind itself along, to
move two steps sideways for every step forwards" (1972:46). I can
hardly improve upon this; the syntax is obviously mobile, even to the
point of hopping. I would want to add, however, that it is so mobile, so
nervous, because *cortaysye* has become more doctrinaire system than
meaningful code for expressing human relations. *Cortaysye* has become, to adapt Spearing's words, an obstacle course for the leisured
and overly refined: Gawain's syntax would not perform such a complicated jig were *cortaysye* less formalized and more relational, less rigorous in relationships and more sensitive to human relations. Gawain
may know in what he is 'praiseworthy' (or 'priced'); he may know
where his 'bounty' lies; but he does not understand the structure of
relation nor does he appreciate the delicate movement of the market
of human affairs. He is indulging a ritual whose meaning he will not
understand until he has been priced and priced in *blood*.

Gawain presumes and presumes upon relation, as does also Arthur's
court. When the Green Knight declines Arthur's invitation to linger at
court, he remarks,

'Bot for þe los of þe, lede, is lyft vp so hyȝe,
And þy burȝ and þy burnes best ar holden,
Stifest vnder stel-gere on stedes to ryde,
Þe wyȝtest and þe worþyest of þe worldes kynde,
Preue for to play wyth in oþer pure laykez,
And here is kydde cortaysye, as I haf herd carp,
And þat hatz wayned me hider, iwyis, at þis tyme.'
                                              (258–64)

The court and its *cortaysye* depend entirely upon references and relation (*kydde . . . as I haf herd carp*), but no one in the court appreciates
just what this means, that each must pay the price of the court's renown. When the court members complain of Arthur's *angardez pryde*

(681) in consenting to Gawain's departure to seek the Green Knight, they conveniently forget that they are as guilty of that pride as Arthur is. They live at court and feed upon its renown. Were Arthur's renown to disappear, they would soon disappear themselves—find excuses to drift away. The courtiers conveniently forget that if the court subsists on renown, it never transcends the experience of relativity and relationship, since renown is a kind of currency, and in that experience it remains always vulnerable to pride. The only way to chasten that pride is to become fully aware of relativity and relationship—to become sensitive to the market of human affairs where references are always necessary. But no one in the court shares this awareness nor this sensitivity—no one has a feel for the structure and the necessity of relation–until Gawain returns from the Green Chapel with the *syngne of surfet* and the *token of vntrawþe* which everyone wears as part (payment) of the *prys* of belonging to the Round Table. Adopting the badge, the court members correct their earlier presumption of relation insofar as they *luflyly acorden* (2514) to wear it. That accord is an agreement, a covenant or convention, which for that very reason is testimony to their consciousness and conscious choice of relation and relationships. Here then is the probable solution to the problem of the discrepancy between Gawain's view of his experience and that of the court (Burrow 1965:158; Spearing 1970:221–22). Of course, the two views differ. That is the point. The court members did not have, nor could they have had, Gawain's experience. They are different from him. But they are affirmed, even reaffirmed, as a community by *his* having had it, and this they celebrate joyously and *luflyly*. Their difference from Gawain is not a lessening of his experience but an affirmation that they and he are relative one to the other even as they are related to each other. Their difference is the motive and the very possibility of their accord. In more senses than one, Gawain has returned with the meaning of Arthur's court.

And this because, in Bertilak's court, as opposed to Arthur's earlier, Gawain is immersed in relation—relativity, prices, *cost(es)*, bargains, and so on—where he becomes *proud of þe prys* that others put on him. Immersed in relation, as if in a sea of troubles, Gawain attempts the coward's way out—so much he himself acknowledges (2374); it is also, he finally realizes, the proud man's way out. If others impose a value on you, do not at all costs disappoint them; if others price your life so high (no matter where you price it), at all costs save your life. At one extreme, Gawain is proud because he presumes and presumes upon relations, and his humility is formality, by rote; at the other extreme, he is proud because he cares too much—is anxious—about relation and relationships: he is proud of himself and his formality, or courtesy, and nobility. At either extreme, however, the sin is the same, the abuse of relationship, or pride—the desire to be complete and self-sufficient when, as a creature made in the image of another, a man is necessarily incomplete and insufficient. All this Gawain eventually does recognize: "'And þus, quen *pryde* schal me pryk for prowes of armes, / Þe loke to þis luf-lace schal *leþe* my hert'" (2437–38; emphasis added). Forced to become a consumer and a merchant while at Hautdesert, forced to consider the commerce of human existence and all that it means, forced to look at himself as one among others to whom he is relative, Gawain *does*, as these two lines prove, learn at last to chasten his pride.

He also learns in this way that he is not absolute. He is not absolutely complete nor is he absolutely incomplete. He is, just like Everyman, in between, in relation to (cf. Burrow's remarks, 1965: 185–86). Gawain is just a man, if a very good man. And as a good man in his world, he is current for *nurture*, for *trawþe*, for *larges*, for *lewté*. To borrow from Augustine, Langland, and Biel, he is coin. Very reliable coin, but coin all the same—relative, measured, and valued. And currency is his condition because he lives in time, the ultimate measure: "A ȝere ȝernes ful ȝerne, and ȝeldez neuer lyke, / Þe forme to þe fynisment foldez ful selden" (498–99). "The yearly changes of seasons, as the Latin encyclopedists tell us, are denominated *curricula* because the seasons run, *quod currunt*" (Silverstein 1968:185). Silverstein's reading of the seasons' passage (491–535) confirms that currency (*quod currunt*), in many forms, is the condition of mortal man: even *Meȝelmas mone* comes *wyth wynter* wage (533; emphasis added; Pace 1969:411, n. 22). Insofar as Gawain insisted on an exclusively private value by *pricing* the green girdle as his life and therefore worth the meaning of his life, or his *larges* and *lewté*, he pridefully attempted to escape the currency of time (death) in which his experience at Hautdesert had immersed him; just as, earlier, in Arthur's court and with Arthur's court, in youthful *surquidré*, he was heedless of the currency of time. But no man can escape this currency, this constant measuring that marks the mutability of the flesh and thus also the distance of the flesh from the ideals to which the spirit aspires. Only the priest, as vicar of the Mediator, can redeem man from time. When the Green Knight absolves Gawain by shriving him (2390–94), he restores Gawain to the debt-free innocence of the baptized infant. He takes Gawain back through time and sets him free to begin again. "[Initium] ut esset, homo creatus est (That a beginning might be, man was created)."[13] Man's chief beauty is that he is a beginning and a source of beginnings, so that mutability, though powerful, does not necessarily reduce him to mere repetition, obsessive cyclings of the same. Hannah Arendt (1958: 236–47) has argued that the promise is man's only hope against the unpredictability of the future and that forgiveness is his only hope against the irreversibility of the past. Gawain makes promises throughout the poem and he is so *trwe* that he almost nullifies the unpredictability of the future; he is almost as good as his word; he is almost as good as his name (cf. 2270–73). But not quite. And so he has to be forgiven. And the Green Knight does forgive him (2390–94), thus reversing the past:

'And I gif þe, sir, þe gurdel þat is golde-hemmed,
For hit is grene as my goune. Sir Gawayn, ʒe maye
Þenk vpon þis ilke þrepe, þer þou forth þryngez
Among prynces of prys, and þis a pure token
Of þe chaunce of þe grene chapel at cheualrous knyʒtez.'
(2395–99)

Henceforth among princes of price, with whom he will compete (*þryngez*), which is to relate to them, Gawain will bear a token, something inherently relative, which will remind him of what he once ignored, the weight (necessarily relative) of the flesh. Wearing this token, he will be free: he will not make the same mistake twice. At no time does he wear the green girdle for *wele* (the point is made twice, see 2037 and 2432); he wears it rather for liberty, although at first he misconstrues the nature of liberty. From the *chaunce of þe grene chapel* on, however, he can enjoy the liberty he desires, the liberty *represented* for him in the girdle, because not making the same mistake twice is as near to liberty as a man is going to get in this life.

4

The New Covenant
of the Green Girdle

i. From Idols to Knots

The previous chapter demonstrated how Gawain is immersed in relationships and relativity during his stay at Hautdesert. Bertilak's Lady seduces him into becoming a consumer and, in the process, exposes his pride and self-regard. Bertilak manipulates him into merchandising and, in the process, exposes his covetousness and legalistic reliance on formality. Involved in Gawain's pride and covetousness alike is the sin of idolatry in which both of these sins are visible and by which they are compounded. Moreover, idolatry and the problems it raises mobilize the poem's consciousness of its textuality.

That Gawain's error is fundamentally the sin of pride no one could reasonably dispute. But, as everyone knows, Gawain himself identifies his sins or errors as *cowarddyse* and *couetyse* (2374).[1] The appearance of conflict here is only an appearance: pride and covetousness are actually intimately related as cause and effect. Like Scripture itself, *Sir Gawain and the Green Knight* understands the origin of sin as double: "Initium omnis peccati superbia (For pride is the beginning of all sin)" (Eccl. 10. 15); "Radix enim omnium malorum est cupiditas (for greed is the root of all evil)" (1 Tim. 6. 10). Pride and greed—greed in its widest sense as any desire for the creation that usurps the desire for the Creator[2]—are cause and effect of every sin inasmuch as the creature, in order to sin, must turn away from the Creator and toward itself (pride), whereupon, having become its own deity, it becomes also its own servant, condemned to desire and yet never to be fulfilled (greed or covetousness). When the creature hands itself over to itself, its only desire from that moment on is itself; therefore, by definition, this desire is greed because it can never be satiated, is infinitely repetitive, and remains stultifyingly mechanical.[3] I do not intend by this analysis to make a judgment—the poem supplies that on its own— rather, a description of what happens to Gawain. When he falls into pride of the price the Lady puts on him, he becomes automatically covetous also. The accompanying emotion of fear (*cowarddyse* and *couetyse*) is simply enough explained. The man who is proud of his life—its price, beauty, glory, what have you—necessarily fears for the loss of that life; and this fear is also the condition of the archetypally covetous man, or the avaricious who fears for the loss of his coin.[4] Pride accompanied by fear leading to covetousness is the degradation that Gawain endures as Bertilak and his Lady expose him to commercial relativity and the subjectivity of pricing.

Proud, cowardly, and covetous, Gawain is also idolatrous. He has deliberately confused the sign and what it signifies. I do not mean 'word' and 'thing': Gawain knows that the words *þe grene gurdel* are not the green girdle. What he does not know, however, and what he deliberately confuses, is the right relationship between the green girdle as sign and what it signifies. For him, the girdle, a piece of cloth, has become identical with his life, so much so that he has paid for it with the meaning of his life, *lewté* and *trawþe*. But this relationship of identity between the green girdle and what it signifies is arbitrary and, in Gawain's case, wholly subjective; and this he ignores. If we think of the green girdle for a moment as a *vox*, then the medieval theory of meaning in language will point out Gawain's oversight instantly:

> Vox non est artata proprie, nisi usus noster accipiendi vocem pro alio est artata ex voluntate et consensu communi circa ipsam. Unde . . . ante impositionem vocis ad significandum requiritur consensus et concordia hominum, et ideo vox non coartatur, nisi quo ad nos. Unde etiam eandem vocem iam impositam possemus imponere de novo ad aliud significandum, si alii vellent mutualiter in hoc concordare.[5]

> There is no contract as to the proper meaning of a word unless our custom of accepting that word instead of another is first agreed upon by our common will and consent. Thus, prior to the imposition of a word to the signifying of something, the consent and concord of men are required; and just so, a word has no proper meaning, unless with regard to us. Thus also the very same word just now imposed to a certain signification we are able to impose anew, to signify something else, if others wish mutually to agree to this.

> Vox potest considerari dupliciter, aut absolute et ante impositionem ad significandum, aut post impositionem. Primo modo po-

test significare oppositum sue significationis, quia voces sunt ad placitum.[6]

A word is able to be considered in two senses, either absolutely and prior to its imposition to the signifying of some thing, or after such imposition. In the first sense, it is able to signify the opposite of its signification [i.e., its ordinary or common meaning], because words are imposed to a signification at the pleasure of those who do the imposing.

The medieval theory understands that meaning enters a *vox* by an *"impositio ad placitum,"* or an arbitrary decision, 'at the pleasure of the impositor'. Gawain ignores this datum even as he proves it by his behavior. He is an idolator because he does not recognize the role of his own arbitrary will in the meaning of the green girdle. To such recognition and the consequent wisdom Gawain must be led if he is to go free of idolatry, covetousness, and pride.

Hence the circumcision. John Burrow (1965:158–59) has already intuited the importance of medieval language theory to *Sir Gawain*, demonstrating that, in the end, back at Arthur's court, the green girdle becomes a sign precisely of human institution, *"ad placitum."* But in his discussion, Burrow fails to emphasize that this is the *third* imposition of meaning on the girdle. The first is Gawain's idolatrous identification of it with his life; the second, which makes the third possible, is his imposition on the girdle of *the syngne of surfet* which follows upon, comes after, the beheading scene or the circumcision. Only after that rite, which is fundamentally significatory and mediatory, does Gawain impose on the girdle a significance that suggests that he understands his earlier error and how to correct it; for if Gawain now names the girdle the *syngne of surfet*, he must also recognize the *excess* of his subjectivity earlier. By undergoing the rite that is strictly a sign, Gawain comes to understand the nature of signs—how arbitrary they are, how easy it is to cut the relationship between them and their signifieds, and, by the same token, how easy it is to tie that relationship in an unbreakable (hence, idolatrous) knot. And his understanding is proved as much by the word *surfet* as by the word *syngne*. Gawain not only sees now that the green girdle is a sign and no more; he also sees that it is a sign of a fault that encompasses both pride and covetousness—excess, in the most basic sense. And from this position, he can go on, we may assume, to see his idolatry since, according to the Christian tradition, covetousness is the source of idolatry. According to St. Paul, "omnis fornicator, aut immundus, aut avarus, quod est idolorum servitus, non habet haereditatem in regno Christi et Dei (no fornicator, or unclean, or covetous person, which is a serving of idols, hath inheritance in the kingdom of Christ and of God)" (Eph. 5. 5). Continuing Paul's teaching, St. Augustine explains that "et ipsa idololatria dicta est avaritia: quia et in ipsa divinitate avarus est, cui non sufficit Deus unus et verus[7] (and idolatry itself is called avarice, because the idolator, for whom the one, true God does not suffice, is also avaricious in matters divine)." Closer in time to *Sir Gawain*, the *Sacrum Commercium Beati Francisci cum Domina Paupertate* (1894:38) also insists that "avaritia . . . est ydolorum servitus, quoniam avarus non implebitur pecunia (avarice . . . is the service of idols, because the avaricious is never satisifed with money)." Finally, a contemporary, John Wyclif, asserts that "et ipsa avaricia . . . est ydolorum servitus, cum omnis talis preponderat temporalia super Deum[8] (avarice itself is the service of idols, because for every avaricious man temporal goods take precedence over God)." The evidence is impressive and makes the point quite forcefully: the degradation from pride accompanied by fear to covetousness involves the self, along every step of the way, in idolatry. Given his response to the green girdle, it is fair to assume that the circumcised Gawain, *accipiens nostram humanitatem*, knows where he has been.

He has been in idolatry because of his insistence on private value to the exclusion of relation and relationships. In theological terms—which we need now to follow the poem's development of the relationship between the green girdle and the pentangle—Gawain elevates a creature to the status of the Creator. The green girdle, a created thing, becomes creative of his life—supposedly it can save his life—and therefore perversely synonymous with the Creator. More importantly, the creature Gawain has become the Creator, Creator of himself. Properly a creature and therefore a sign of chivalric ideals, Gawain in his confusion comes to think that he is the Creator of the ideal—that he is chivalry itself. Properly a particular instance, Gawain comes to believe himself the source, since, for example, he can determine that accepting the green girdle is chivalrous. Or, again, a particular instance of chivalric ideals not only might but also probably would fail when a *prynces of pris depreses hym so þikke* between betrayal of the *teccheles termes of talkyng noble* and betrayal of his host through adultery (see 1770, 917). For a mortal, fallible, particular man, there is no way out of this predicament. Gawain, however, assumes that he must honor the Lady in *luf-talkyng* and his host in the duties owed him by a guest. More, Gawain assumes that he *can* honor them both. After all, he *is* Gawain, the *fyne fader of nurture* (emphasis added)—as it were, the deity of *nurture*. Gawain becomes so engrossed in *being* chivalry that finally he forgets to practice chivalry, and accepts the green girdle. Gawain so identifies himself with chivalry, the ideal, especially since the Lady will not stop insisting on as much, that he forgets that he is only a particular instance of chivalry, only *a* chivalrous man. But by forgetting that he is a man, Gawain leaves himself open and vulnerable to the human. The human wants to live. The human Gawain cannot be the ideal Gawain who is chivalry. The human wants to live—names and ideals be damned.

Gawain's liberation from idolatry—his restoration to full consciousness of his mediate, transitory, creaturely status—does not occur until the circumcision. But at that moment, Gawain *does* impose upon the girdle the *syngne of surfet*, where *surfet* is effectively a confession of sin. At that moment, Gawain enters into and accepts the mortal inheritance of signification and mediation—which is to say, the inheritance of the Fall and of the incompleteness resulting from it. Now, as Gawain imposes significance on the green girdle, it comes to replace the pentangle as his emblem. And it does so because the pentangle is the most treacherous idol in the poem—most treacherous precisely because it is the creature in the poem apparently most innocent of such perversion.

The poem reports the history of the pentangle thus: [9]

> Hit is a syngne þat Salamon set sumquyle
> In bytoknyng of trawþe, bi tytle þat hit habbez,
> For hit is a figure þat haldez fyue poyntez,
> And vche lyne vmbelappez and loukez in oþer,
> And ayquere hit is endelez; and Englych hit callen
> Oueral, as I here, þe endeles knot.   (625–30)

John Burrow (1965:188–89) has discussed this passage in light of late medieval sign theory, and he will repay quotation at some length here:

> The sign does not rest on [Solomon's] authority alone, since this is a case of 'imposito secundum naturam'. The relation between the moral concept truth and the geometrical figure is not merely arbitrary, like the relation between that concept and the various *verbal* signs which denote it ('truth', 'veritas', 'loiauté', etc.); it is natural, because, as Solomon was the first to see, the pentangle is of its nature *like* truth—or so the poet claims. Both are fivefold, interlocking, 'endless'. The pentangle is a kind of geometrical 'picture' of truth, in fact, and so has a natural right or 'title' to its

signification – it was possible [in the Middle Ages] to argue that many words did have a qualified 'title' to their signification insofar as they could be shown, by 'etymology', to describe, or at least say something not too inappropriate about their referents.

I can hardly improve upon these words. But I do want to extend their import. The crux of the matter is the natural sign's entitlement. Even in a world that insists on the subjectivity of value, some signs are, on a scale of the conventional to the natural, closer to natural than to conventional, just as the value of gold is closer to natural than to conventional, although at the same time the value of gold obviously depends on the market. And *Sir Gawain and the Green Knight* exploits this fact in order to expose the threat of idolatry in every natural sign. Precisely because the pentangle is more natural than most signs, precisely because it is so close to its signified—so entitled—the pentangle can all too easily obscure the distance or, better, the difference between itself as sign and what it signifies. I am *not* claiming that the pentangle *is* (inherently) an idol—obviously it is not so for the poet—but that it can be perverted into an idol quite easily because of its natural or entitled relation to its signified. He who bears the pentangle can all too easily presume *to own* the significance of the pentangle. He can all too easily presume to appropriate the proper, and the property, of the sign, namely ideal Christian chivalry, which is always already elsewhere.[10] Burrow (1965:159) himself writes that

> by breaking down Gawain's 'truth' [the Green Knight] has demonstrated that no one, not even a knight of Arthur's court, can justly claim the pentangle as his emblem. The adventure has, in fact, established a strong *a fortiori* proof of the old doctrine of original sin.

Indeed, no one in Arthur's court is worthy to bear the shield because no one's mortal part can withstand the desire to own the significance of the shield. It is as if in bearing the shield a knight would become the shield. But this is not the way to put on the armor of God; the temper (and the tenor) of that armor is always elsewhere.

So it is precisely that the green girdle replaces the pentangle (never again mentioned in the poem after its introduction). The green girdle, as Burrow rightly insists, is an arbitrary sign: it is a mere wisp of cloth with no immemorial reputation. The significance of the green girdle can only be imposed *ad placitum*; there can be no question of its having any special title to its significance. To be sure, when he first appropriates it, Gawain absolutizes its significance *ad placitum*. He absolutizes his own subjective pleasure. But this he does because in his pride, cowardice, and covetousness, he has already fallen into idolatry. The weight of the pentangle has, as it were, already taken its toll on his mortal part: he has presumed to be the ideal of chivalry rather than accept his status as a particular instance of chivalry. As an idolator, Gawain is all too prone to identify his life, the signified, with the green girdle, its sign. And so it is that he must undergo a rite, fundamentally significatory and mediatory, instituted against idolatry. The rite of circumcision cuts the false identity between sign and signified even as it restores Gawain to his human inheritance of mediation. And because that identity is cut as also because Gawain is restored, the green girdle becomes again what in fact it was all along, a sign, imposed *ad placitum*, the *syngne of surfet*, and the *token of vntrawþe*.

The kind of idolatrous misappropriation of which Gawain is guilty and because of which he presumes, although almost unconsciously, to be literally the *fyne fader of nurture*, overwhelms him not only in the pentangle and the green girdle but also in the textuality of knighthood and chivalry. At one point in her effort, as part of the *gomen* to humble Gawain, to enmesh him in commercial relativity, Bertilak's Lady sweetens her flattery with the hint, though just the barest hint, that Gawain is the *author* of knighthood and chivalry. She never comes out and says this; that would be gross and uncouth. But she does let it hang in the air. Asking Gawain for the *skyl* (1509) why, when he is the *knyȝt comlokest kyd of* [his] *elde* (1520), she has "'neuer of [his] hed helde no wordez / Þat euer longed to luf, lasse ne more'" (1523–24), the Lady interrupts her question to remark:

'And of alle cheualry to chose, þe chef þyng alosed
Is þe *lel layk of luf*, þe lettrure of armes;
For to telle of þis teuelyng of þis trwe knyȝtez,
Hit is *þe tytelet token and tyxt of her werkkez*,
How ledes for her lele luf hor lyuez han auntered,
Endured for her drury dulful stoundez,
And after wenged with her walour and voyded her care,
And broȝt blysse into boure with bountees hor awen.'
                    (1512–19; emphasis added)

The token and the text of the works of knights are entitled just as the pentangle signifies *bi tytle þat hit habbez*. Hence, like the pentangle, this token and this text—the *lettrure of armes*, the *lel layk of luf*—can obscure the difference between themselves as signs and the *teuelyng* that they signify. Because of their natural relation to the deeds of knights, this token and this text can supplant and replace those deeds. The natural relation consists in the extreme formalism of both texts or letters and arms: both are highly decorous; both exclude the mere dross of existence; both idealize and rigorize messy experience; both suppress the contingent and rationalize the random; both structure the adventurous ("that which is about to come") into predictable and answerable style.[11] Because of such a title, the textuality of knighthood can become an icon, an absolute form, impervious to experience and innocent of the contingency of matter. The iconicity of this textuality repudiates the fallen and the fallible—the mortal: instead of a sweaty, clanking knight aching for a bath (and perhaps for a green girdle), there is the formal beauty of a literary paragon. Where there is text, what need of a subject?

But the title of the text can be revoked. The natural relation between textuality and reality can be questioned, it can be criticized. And what of (literary) criticism? It sub-jects the text to the temporality and the humanity of interpretation. It re-opens the question of the text's relation to reality. It initiates again the process of mediation. It insists on experience, on the random, on the unpredictable. It humanizes the text as it re-institutes the crisis of the human—the fallen, the fallible, the particular. It bears the text back, it refers the text, to reality.

Hence Gawain's *refusal* to criticize, to gloss, to *expoun* the text:

> 'Bot to take þe toruayle to myself to trwluf *expoun*,
> And towche þe temez of *tyxt* and talez of armez
> To yow þat, I wot wel, weldez more *sly3t*
> Of þat *art*, bi þe half, or a hundreth of seche
> As I am, oþer euer schal, in erde þer I leue,
> Hit were a folé felefolde, my fre, by my trawþe.'
> (1540–45; emphasis added)

Burrow (1965:92) has observed how "bookish" the Lady's digression into the textuality of knighthood is; it is romantic, as it were, in the adolescent sense of the word. But that is a careful ploy on her part. She means to seem young and innocent so that Gawain, slightly puffed up, one must say, can respond with his own bit of flattery by adopting the stance of all authors who never expound their own works. Gawain's extraordinarily polite reluctance *to trwluf expoun* suggests that the Lady has succeeded in letting him feel as if he had written the book on chivalry and is now far too polite to display his learning.

But this polite reluctance has another, deeper motive which the Lady is also seeking. If Gawain were *to trwluf expoun* and *towche þe temez of tyxt and talez of armez*, he would, in the very gloss, betray the difference between himself—a particular, fallen, mortal knight—and the ideal knighthood inscribed in the *lettrure of armes*. As I have demonstrated elsewhere, the gloss temporalizes, humanizes, particularizes the text; the gloss refers the text to reality (Shoaf 1975:50). If Gawain glosses the text, he concedes that he is not the text—that he is not formal, decorous, and iconic. He is not stable and eternal as letters are; he is mutable and temporal as men are. And this concession is repugnant to Gawain, proud as he is of the price the Lady has put on him. Gawain does not want to concede his humility (though the Lady and her cohorts are forcing him to); he does not want to enter into his inheritance of mediation. Gawain would prefer to be a text, an *auctoritas*, so entitled to its referent that rather than signify the referent, and therefore suffer the crisis of mediation, it would *be* the referent—author and text, father and son, Lord and creature in one. Little wonder Gawain undergoes circumcision at the Green Knight's hands; he is a proud, cowardly, covetous, and idolatrous man. At the same time, he is the *knyȝt comlokest kyd of* [his] *elde*.

If the best of all possible knights is after all an imperfect man, it follows that the best of all *tytelet tokens and tyxts of* [knight's] *werkkez*, being the works of man, might also be imperfect. And the *Gawain*-poet knows this. He is himself, of course, writing a *tytelet token and tyxt*, a *lettrure of armes*, in the text we are reading. He, however, invites and welcomes criticism of his text, in part because, as Larry D. Benson (1965:207–8) has demonstrated, "the subject of this romance is romance itself," and in part to prepare his text so that its "title" to "reality" never becomes a misappropriation of "reality." And one major element in this preparation of his text is the repudiation of its own iconicity.

If the *lel layk of luf* is a lettrure *of armes* and if the pentangle is a figure of which *vche lyne vmbelappez and* loukez *in oþer*, the poem itself is a "stori stif and stronge, / With *lel letteres loken*" (34–35; emphasis added). The poem, like the *layk of luf*, being a lettered thing, is also a *lettrure*, or 'learning'; moreover, its letters are *lel* just like the *layk of luf*; finally, the *lel letteres* of the poem are *locked* just like the lines of the pentangle. Hence the form of the poem repeats itself in the pentangle and the *lettrure of armes*: the poem analyzes its own form and repositions the three differentiae of that form—*lel, lettrure, loukez*—in seams of its structure where iconicity and idolatry are in crisis, in need of critical interruption. In doing so, the poem acknowledges that its own form, potentially iconic and idolatrous, is also in crisis—in need of critical interruption, questioning, and interpretation.[12]

Criticized, questioned, interrupted, the poem formally can never become an icon. It cannot by any title claim to own the reality to which it refers. The poem can only be a sign. A green girdle.

In replacing the pentangle with the green girdle, the poem is careful to repeat the word *knot* twice:

> Þenne he kaȝt to þe *knot*, and þe kest lawsez. . . .
>   (2376; emphasis added)

> Loken vnder his lyfte arme, þe lace, with a *knot*,
> In tokenyng he watz tane in tech of a faute.
>   (2487–88; emphasis added)

The pentangle, because of its peculiar form, is *þe endeles knot* (630):

> Þerfore on his schene schelde schapen watz þe *knot*
> Ryally wyth red golde vpon rede gowlez,
> Þat is þe pure pentaungel wyth þe peple called
>   with lore.   (662–65; emphasis added)

The green girdle replaces the pentangle because, unlike the latter, it forms a knot that can be loosened. The *knot* that the green girdle *as sign* ties with what it signifies is not permanent, fixed, or geometrically perfect. The green girdle, as the poem is careful to emphasize, is a *pure token* (2398)—its token-ness, if you will, free of all prescription and proscription. The knot that it as sign ties is the mortal knot, *ad placitum*, of mediation. This sign, this knot, comes with no prescribed meaning; no meaning is even already implied (as by a geometrical shape). This sign "means" only as you tie and untie it—this sign tells you who you are, by how you use it. And when the poem repudiates the iconicity of the pentangle, to assimilate itself to the green girdle, such is the *knot* that it turns to tie.[13]

ii. *Hony soyt qui mal pence*

Gawain wears back to Arthur's court the mortal knot of mediation. The experience of this knot, of its being tied, is humbling and productive of humility. At Arthur's court, however, in a sense, the *superbum Ilium (Aeneid* 2. 2–3) of Aeneas and *Felix Brutus* (13) has never fallen (see intro. at n. 4). It has continued in the *surquidré* of the court of Arthur, Brutus's descendant. But that *surquidré* is at least interrupted, if not chastened, by Gawain's new knowledge, or, say, his new self. Upon his return, Gawain *ferlyly telles* (2494) the company his adventures and *biknowez alle þe* costes *of care þat he hade* (2495; emphasis added). Again, it would demean the poem not to hear the homonym. Now Gawain not only 'confesses the hardships' that he suffered; he also 'knows the cost'—the cost of his experience, the cost of his *lewté* and *trawþe*, the cost of himself. Gawain brings back to Arthur's court a knowledge of man's incompleteness—*þe faut and þe fayntyse of þe flesche crabbed*—and man's consequent need of relation. No longer a youthful idealist, Gawain is now a mature steward of the ideal. As such, he knows the price of the ideal because he knows the weight of mortality: "'For mon may hyden his harme, bot vnhap ne may hit, / For þer hit onez is tachched twynne wil hit neuer'" (2511–12). Gawain knows the price of idealism—to strive and ever fall short. And the court is sensitive to Gawain's knowledge. They *luflyly acorden* to wear the *token of vntrawþe* and in that new convention, instituted *ad placitum*, they confess that all human ideals are ultimately *untrue*. But. (The structure of *Sir Gawain and the Green Knight* always necessitates our return to "but.") In that very confession, they also witness, *luflyly*, that the negative is a positive[14]—that *trawþe* exists if it is known, known by man in this world, through (the mediation of) its negative. And their witness—their comfortable display of the negative (the green girdle)—is a rebuke to the proud.

Which is why some reader of the poem appended *Hony soyt qui mal pence* to the manuscript: he understood the poem to say, "Let the shame be to him who thinks a sign or token of humility is humiliating or shameful." Whoever added the Order of the Garter's motto to the manuscript of *Sir Gawain* had read his poem and read it well. He had grasped that the green girdle is a *sign* that translates (*translatio*) the empire (*imperii*)[15] without the pride (*superbia*)—the sign of a kingdom that knows its place.

Appendix:
Vocabulary of Commercial Words

The table is compiled from the Tolkien-Gordon-Davis edition of *Sir Gawain and the Green Knight*. The order is alphabetical; the etymologies, included for the sake of historical comparison, are those in the T-G-D glossary. Line number(s) in *SGGK* follow the etymology. The numbers in the right margin indicate the frequency of a word's occurrence in a commercial sense. They are not necessarily the frequency of the word's occurrence generally. Moreover, several of the words have their commercial sense only in their context in the poem: *euen* and *losse* are good examples. Finally, since some words are so obvious in their meaning as to need no comment, no attempt is made in the text to discuss every word or every occurrence of each word.

The issues of context and of frequency of occurrence in a commercial sense point to a serious problem. An inevitable residue of subjectivity remains in any compilation of a specialized vocabulary. No two people would compile quite the same commercial vocabulary or sexual vocabulary or political vocabulary or other kind of vocabulary. Recognizing this problem, I have tried to err on the side of *exclusion*— there are many more words in the poem that I think are commercial than I list here—on the assumption that only words a majority of readers can and will consider commercial are logically admissible. Doubtless I have still managed to include some words that many, perhaps most, would debate, but I trust these are a minority. And even were there a dozen such debatable entries, the vocabulary is still impressively large, obviously important.

Frequency of
occurrences in
a commercial sense

acheue: OFr. *achever*; 1107	1
as(s)ay: OFr. *essayer*; 2362, 2457	2
bargayn: OFr. *bargaine*; 1112	1
bounté: OFr. *bo(u)nté*: 357, 1519	2
busy: OE. *bysigian*; 1066	1
busyly: from OE. *bysig*; 1824	1
busynes: OE. *bysignes*; 1840	1
chaffer: OE. *cēap* + *faru*; cp. ON. kaupför; 1647, 1939	2
charres: OE. *cerr, cær*; 1674	1
chaunge: OFr. *cha(u)ng(i)er*; 1107, 1406, 1678	3
chepe *n.*: OE. *cēap*; 1939, 1940, 1941	3
chepen *v.*: OE. *cēapian*; 1271	1
cheue: OFr. *chevir* and *achever*; 1271, 1390	2
cheuisaunce: OFr. *chevissa(u)nce*; 1390, 1406, 1678, 1939	4
cost: late OE. *cost* from ON. *kostr*; 546, 750, 943–45, 1269–72, 1483, 1849, 2360, 2495	8
couenaunt: OFr. *covena(u)nt*; 393, 1123, 1384, 1408, 1642, 2242, 2328, 2340	8
couetyse: OFr. *coveitise*; 2374, 2380, 2508	3
dawed: OE. *dugan*; 1805	1
dele: OE. *dǣlan*; 295, 397, 452, 1114, 1266, 1662, 1752, 1805, 2285, 2449	10
deserue: OFr. *deservir*; 452, 1779, 1803	3
disert: OFr. *desert*; 1266	1
ernde: OE. *ǣrende*; ON. *erendi*; 1051, 1067, 2303	3
euen: OE. *efen, efne*; 1266, 1641	2
fech: OE. *fetian, feccan*; 1857	1
fee: OFr. *f(i)e, fieu*; 1622	1
foch(che): var. of *fech*, cf. OE. *feotian* or *fatian*; 396	1
forfete: OFr. *forfait, -fet*; 2394	1
forȝelde: OE. *forgéldan*; 839, 1279, 1535, 2429	4
forward(e): OE. *foreweard*; 378, 409, 1105, 1395, 1405, 1636, 1934, 2347	8
fraunchis(e): OFr. *fra(u)nchise*; 1264	1
gayn *adj.*: ON. *gegn, adj.*; 1241	1
gayn(e) *v.*: ON. *gegna*; 584, 1829	2
gayne *n.*: OFr. *gaaigne*; 2349	1

Frequency

garysoun: OFr. *gariso(u)n*, infl. in sense by ON. *gersumi*;
        1255, 1807, 1837   3
gif: ON. *gefa, gifa*; 2349   1
gift(e):   ON. *gift*; 1799, 1807, 1822, 2030   4
god(e):   OE. *gōd n.*; 1064, 1944, 2031, 2127   4
gold(e):   OE. *góld*; 1255, 1837, 2150   3
ȝelde: OE. *géldan*; 1038, 1215, 1263, 1292, 1963, 2056, 2410,
        2441   8
ȝolden: *ppl.* of preceding word; 453   1
halde: OE. *háldan*; 1040, 1828   2
iuel: OFr. *joel*; 1856   1
larges(se):   OFr. *largece, -esse*; 2381   1
losse: OE. *los*; 2507   1
nedez: OE. *nēd*; 2216   1
note: OE. *notu*; 358   1
oghe: OE. *āgan, āhte*; 1526, 1941   2
pay *n.*:   OFr. *paie*; 2247   1
paye *v.*:   OFr. *payer*; 1941, 1945, 2341   3
penyes: OE. *peni(n)g*; 79   1
prayse: OFr. *preis(i)er*; 356, 913, 1228, 1630, 1633, 1850,
        2072   7
prys: OFr. *pris*; 79, 912, 1247, 1249, 1277, 1379, 1630, 1770,
        1850, 1945, 2364, 2398   12
profered: OFr. *parofrir*; AN. *prof(e)rir*, infl. by *pro-*; 2346,
        2350   2
quyt-clayme: OFr. *quiter, ppl.* + *clayme*; 293   1
quyte: OFr. *quiter*; 2244, 2324   2
relece: OFr. *relaiss(i)er, reless-*; 2342   1
remnaunt: OFr. *remena(u)nt*; 2342   1
renne: ON. *renna*; 310, 2458   2
restore: OFr. *restorer*; 2283, 2354   2
rewarde: ONFr. *reward*; 1804   1
rich(e):   OE. *rīce*; OFr. *riche*; 1646, 1744, 1827   3
spede *n.*:   OE. *spēd*; 918   1
spede *v.*:   OE. *(ge)spēdan*; 2216   1
spende: OE. *spéndan*; 410, 2113   2
swap: same as ME. *swappen*, "strike"; 1108   1
tyde: OE. *tīdan*; 1396   1
vnworþi: OE. *unweorþe*; 1244, 1835   2

	Frequency
wage: ONFr. *wage*; 396, 533	2
wele: OE. *wela*; 7, 1270, 1394, 1820, 2037, 2432	6
wynne *n*.: OE. *gewinn*; 2420	1
wynne *v*.: OE. *ge-winnan* - ON. *vinna*; 984, 1106, 1379, 1386, 1394, 1550, 2091, 2415	8
worth: OE. *weorþ(e)*, *wyrþe*; 1269, 1820	2
worþy: OE. *wyrþig*, "merited" infl. by *wyrþe*, "worth(y)"; 261, 559, 819, 1477, 1848	5
	189

Notes

The Abbreviations list begins on page ix.

Introduction

1. Line numbers for all quotations of *SGGK* are from the T-G-D 1967 edition reprinted in 1968 with corrections.
2. Numerous scholars have noted and discussed the commercial imagery in *SGGK*. The following discussions have been most helpful to me: Burrow 1965:83, 134; Heinzelman 1980:36, 286–87; Pace 1969:404–11; Tamplin 1969:408, 418–19; Taylor 1971:1–15.
3. For an informative history of the word 'economy,' see Singer 1958:29–57; for the meaning of *dispensatio*, frequent and crucial in Scripture, see Chenu 1968:168–70.
4. On the role of *superbum Ilium* (*Aeneid* 3. 2–3) in *SGGK*, see David 1968:402–9; Kaske 1979; Silverstein 1965:189–206.
5. This formulation indicates my pervasive debt in reading the poem to Benson 1965 and Burrow 1965.

Chapter 1

1. Du Boulay (1970) offers a lucid and informative demonstration of this phenomenon. Also helpful are Tigar and Levy 1977:1–187.
2. For a discussion of the analogy of proper proportionality, the use of which in the pricing of Gawain argues not only for his mortal limits but also for ours—his and our relativity and dependence on relationships—see Ross 1969:99–138, especially pp. 102 and 129.
3. On the shield, see Ackerman 1958:265; Burrow 1965:189; Englehardt 1955:255; Friedman and Osberg 1977:301–15, especially pp. 314–15; Green 1962:121–39 (reprinted in Blanch 1966:176–94); Kaske 1979; Malarkey and Toelken 1964:19–20 (reprinted in Howard and Zacher 1968:243–44); Taylor 1974:13.
4. Consult Blenkner 1977:357; Kaske 1979; and also, though with extreme caution, Schnyder 1961:59–60.
5. It would be possible and also, I believe, helpful to express this perception in terms of the Pelagian controversy. As we know, this controversy was alive and strenuous in the fourteenth century; Bradwardine's efforts to renew Augustinism are sufficient proof of that (see for a convenient overview Oberman 1978:80–93). Indeed, as Oberman clearly demonstrates,

81

by the 1330s a new florescence of Augustinian teaching and feeling was evident. In this context, Gawain and, indeed, all of Arthur's court, can be seen as Pelagians, or the sort who presume themselves sufficient to do and to be good; the Green Knight, however, challenges this and all the other presumptions of Arthur's world, and when Gawain returns from the Green Chapel, he returns convinced of the "faut and þe fayntyse of þe flesche crabbed / How tender hit is to entyse teches of fylþe" (2435–36)—which is indisputably an Augustinian conviction, the sense of one who has learned the limitations to human striving. (See also chap. 4 at n. 15.)

6. My formulation again looks to the Pelagian controversy. In strict Augustinian terms, Gawain cannot *merit* anything without the prior infusion of grace. That grace has been given to him is, of course, obvious; in one very real sense, the Green Knight is evidence of as much (see Prov. 3. 12; Heb. 12. 6). But until his confrontation with the Green Knight, Gawain does not actually appreciate that all his efforts must come to naught without grace; only through his experience at the Green Chapel does he discover the humility that enables him to try to merit his name.

7. *Sermo* 329. 1 (PL 38:1454), as quoted in Riviére 1933:106.

8. Emphasis added, *Sermo* 130. 2 (PL 38:726) as quoted in Herz 1958:206.

9. Emphasis added, *Enarrationes in Psalmos* 30. 2 (CCSL 38:192); Herz 1958:79.

10. Following is a partial listing of instances of commercial imagery and rhetoric in Augustine's works: *Enarrationes in Psalmos* 148. 8 (CCSL 40: 2170), Herz 1958:204–5; *Sermones* 80. 5 (PL 38:496–97), Herz 1958: 197–98; 90. 10 (PL 38:566); 124. 4 (PL 38:688), Herz 1958:206; 158. 2 (PL 38:863), Hamm 1977:9; *Contra Epistulam Parmeniani* 1. 7. 12 (CSEL 51:31), Herz 1958:211; *In Johannis Euangelium* 13. 14 (CCSL 36:138), Herz 1958: 216; also 40. 9 (CCSL 36:355–56). Consider also the following example from St. Ambrose: "Neminem jugo servitutis astrictum possidet [sc. diabolus], nisi se prius peccatorum aere ei vendiderit (The devil owns no one bound under the yoke of slavery to him unless that person first sells himself to him for the coins, the price, of sin)"; *De Jacob et Vita Beata* 1. 3 (PL 14:602–3).

11. For a convenient collection of examples, see Javelet 1967:2, 63, n. 190; see also Boethius, *Philosophiae Consolatio* 5. 3. 34 and 35 and the commentary by Mohrmann 1976:55–58; *Piers the Plowman* C. 18. 72–81 and the commentary by Raw 1969:143–79, especially pp. 156–57 and 337–38; Häring 1955:508–12 and 1956:46–49; finally, Riehle 1981: 101–3.

12. Out of the numerous economic histories of medieval Europe in general and England in particular, I have found the following most useful: Bernard 1972:274–338; Bridbury 1962; de Roover 1967 and 1971; Duby 1974 and 1976; Heers 1973; Kershaw 1976:85–132; Lopez 1976; Miskimin 1969; Murphy 1973; Pirenne 1937; Postan 1972 and 1973:41–48, 186–213; Rörig 1967:111–12, 161–89; Spicciani 1977.

13. Lopez 1976:156–57. Murray (1978:60) lucidly describes the abstract prin-

ciple of this phenomenon: "Among forms of wealth money combines a peculiar group of qualities. By a mechanism as mysterious as its results are unmistakable, analogous qualities appear in societies where money circulates. The qualities of money have been enumerated: it moves freely from hand to hand; it travels; it divides almost anyhow; a lot fits in a small space; it can be left to pile up without suffering natural vicissitudes. These qualities are reflected in societies with money in them. Men's mutual relations shift, as if liquified by their medium of exchange; *men* travel; social blocks split, like sums of cash, into changeable groupings of individuals; people herd in towns, like coins in a chest; and power, finally, like value, is increasingly abstracted from the perishable to the imperishable, from individuals to institutions. A simple formula captures this whole effect: liquidity in wealth makes for social liquidity; abstraction in wealth makes for an abstraction of power." Consult further on this crucial phenomenon Foucault 1971:168—95 and Sohn-Rethel 1978:13—79.

14. That covetousness and avarice are synonymous in Middle English is evidenced by Chaucer's *Pardoner's Tale* VI C: 423—24.

Chapter 2

1. Schnyder (1961:44—45) also notes the general relevance of the Feast of the Circumcision to the events of the poem, but his information is meager, his ideology suspect, and his interpretations correspondingly weak.
2. The conclusion to *Pearl*, lines 1209—10, most vividly illustrates his devotion to the liturgy.
3. Cabrol, DACL 3:2:1717—28, especially 1718; see also Weiser 1952:135—40.
4. Emphasis added, Mirk 1905:45; see also Tamplin 1969:418—19.
5. See Blenkner 1977:371—72; Burrow 1965:104—10; Spearing 1970:225—27.
6. The Venerable Bede, *Homelia* 11 (CCSL 122:74—75); and for the "prima praevaricatio" and the "pactum" both, see also Angelomus of Luxueil, *Commentarius in Genesin* 17. 15 (PL 115:181) and Rupert of Deutz, *In Genesim* 5. 33 (CCCM 21:368).
7. The antiphon was current in England in *The Hereford Breviary* 1904:182; *The Sarum Breviary* 1879:1,292; and the *York Breviary* 1880:143; it was also current in Old English as no. 12, lines 1—6, of *The Advent Lyrics of the Exeter Book* 1959:77. Herz (1958:24—52) in his study of the origin and the dissemination of the antiphon dates it to the fifth century A.D.
8. Amalarius, *Liber officialis* 4. 32, 1948:505—9; Sicard of Cremona, *Mitrale* 5. 7 (PL 213:225—33); Prepositinus of Cremona, *Tractatus de Officiis* 1. 48, 1969:38—39; Durandus 1570:fol. 278v—280r.
9. Consider further Bede's explanation of why Christ was circumcised (*Homelia* 11 in CCSL 122:74):

Et ut nobis necessarium oboediendi uirtutem praecipuo commandaret exemplo factum sub lege filium suum misit Deus in mundum; non quia ipse legi quicquam debeat quia unus magister noster unus est legislator et iudex sed ut eos qui sub lege positi legis onera portare nequiuerant sua conpassione iuuaret ac de servili conditione quae sub lege erat ereptos in adoptionem filiorum quae per gratiam est *sua largitate reduceret*. Suscepit igitur circumcisionem lege decretam in carne.

And in order that He might enjoin upon us the necessary virtue of obedience by an outstanding example, God sent His Son into the world, Himself subject to the Law; not because He owes anything to the Law, of course, since alone and uniquely He is our master, our law-giver, and our judge, but in order that those living under the Law, who were nevertheless unable to bear the burden of the Law, He might console and aid by His compassion, and in order that from their servile condition which obtained under the Law, He might, once they were taken up into the adoption of sons, which is through grace, *free them through His largesse*. Therefore, He endured the circumcision in the flesh which is decreed by Law. (emphasis added)

10. The most famous instances in Middle English poetry of Christ as a knight are doubtless those in *Piers the Plowman*—see especially B. 18. 19—35.
11. *To compare* is both 'to set in relation to' and 'to price'—see DL-FAC 1954: 179, s.v. "1 comparo" and "2 comparo"—and the double meaning neatly summarizes the Green Knight's treatment of Gawain.
12. So Augustine, *Contra Julianum Pelagianum* 6. 20 (PL 44:834). He will also see in the *luf-lace* or *syngne of surfet* (2433) precisely that *superfluitas* that, according to numerous commentators, circumcision cuts away: in addition to the passage from St. Gregory (chap. 2 after n. 10), see Ambrose, *Epistola* 78 (PL 16:1268); also his *De Abraham* 2. 11. 78 (PL 14:494) and 2. 11. 84 (PL 14:496); pseudo-Bede, *In Pentateuchum Commentarii—Genesis 17* (PL 91:237); St. Bernard, "In Circumcisione Domini" 2 (PL 183:135); Hugh of St. Cher 1669:7, fol. 143r; Marius Victorinus, *Commentariorum in Genesin Libri tres* 3 (PL 61:965).
13. On the 'character' or σφραγίς imprinted by baptism, see Lampe 1951: 154—55.
14. So *Pearl*, lines 639—40: "Oure forme fader hit [blysse parfyt] con *for-fete* / Þurȝ an apple þat he vpon con byte" (emphasis added).
15. See Petrus Lombard, *In Epistolam ad Romanos* 6. 6—11 (PL 191:1404); Thomas Aquinas, ST 3a. 69. 3; and Lottin 1954:4, 304—5.
16. Richard of St. Victor (ascribed by Migne to Hugh of St. Victor), *Sermo* 49 (PL 177:1035—36); see also Durandus 1570:fol. 280r.
17. Honorius Augustodunensis, *Sacramentarium* 93, "De Circumcisione Domini et Epiphania" (PL 172:798); see further Honorius Augustodunensis's *Speculum Ecclesiae*, "In Octavis Domini" (PL 172:842); also Bede, *Homelia* 11 (CCSL 122:77—78); pseudo-Bede, *Genesis 17* (PL 91:237); Hugh of St. Cher 1669:7, fol. 143r; Ludolph of Saxony 1729:46b; Gorham, fol. 63va; Petrus Cantor, "Summa Abel," fol. 17r.

18. I have relied on the following studies: in addition to Courtenay 1971: 96–102 and Hamm 1977:407–10; also Courtenay 1972:185–209 and 1972–1973:275–95; Oberman 1977:165–70, 211–14; and finally Ozment 1980: 35–36.

19. See ST 3a. 62. 1 *ad resp.* and 3a. 64. 1, for examples of this common phrase.

20. Emphasis added; Augustine, *De Nuptiis et Concupiscentia* 2. 11 (PL 44:450); see further Rupert of Deutz, *In Genesim* 5. 31 (CCCM 21:365–66); also ST la. 2 ae. 101, art. 2 and the commentary by Chydenius 1960:36.

21. This is basic Pauline doctrine: "and he [Abraham] received the sign of circumcision, a seal of the justice of the faith, which he had, being uncircumcised; that he might be the father of all them that believe, being uncircumcised" (Rom. 4. 11). All the exegetes I have been able to consult agree with and repeat the Pauline emphasis: see, for a few from among many examples, Aegidius Romanus 1554/1555:fol. 28v; Augustine, *De Gratia Christi et de Peccato Originali* 30 (PL 44:402); Bede, *Homelia* 11 (CCSL 122:75); Durandus 1570:fol. 278v; Hugh of St. Cher 1669:7, fol. 159r; Petrus Lombard, *Sententiarum Libri Quattor* 4. 1. 6 (PL 192:840).

22. ST 3a. 70. 2 ad resp. 1; and the Feast itself is celebrated, we remember, on a day when the Church is particularly militant against idolatry (see chap. 1 at n. 3).

Chapter 3

1. For the currency of the double meaning of *prayse* in the late Middle Ages, see *Catholicon Anglicum* 1881:289–90 and notes.

2. Although the T-G-D edition (1967:109) notes that "*of fyne force* is a conventional term which long remained in legal use," it is difficult to imagine that this convention completely muted the other, *fin'amors* convention, itself certainly a venerable system of ideas and terms.

3. The MED's examples of *bisinesse* in the commercial sense generally derive from the very late fourteenth or early fifteenth century, the likely date of composition for *SGGK*—see B:903–4.

4. That gold has desirable properties—such as malleability, ductility, durability—I hardly deny; but these inherent properties are not values. Rather they are valued; and though all may agree that they should have value, few would agree on *how much* value since there is no telling (throughout human history) what a man or woman will do for gold.

5. For an enlightening and an exact account of the resurgence of covenantal theology in the fourteenth century, see Courtenay 1971:118–19.

6. Cf. the discussion of the fortune of 'convention' in Williams 1976:70–71; see also Tigar and Levy 1977:145.

7. The *Gawain*-poet's fascination with the Old Testament and with questions of the Law is well illustrated by *Patience* and *Cleanness*; see also the commentary in Spearing 1970:79–95.

8. These remarks are based on the exegesis of Romans 6. 23, which consistently stresses, among other issues, that the "stipendia peccati" are *owed* to

the sinner, because he and they are within the sphere of nature, whereas grace is free—precisely gratuitous—and unmerited because no one is "worth" the mercy of God; see Abélard, *Commentaria in Epistolam Pauli ad Romanos* 3. 6 (CCCM 11:186–87); Aegidius Romanus 1554/1555:fol. 41r; Augustine, *Enchiridion ad Laurentium de Fide et Spe et Caritate* 28. 107 (CCSL 46:107); and the *Glossa Ordinaria* 1588:6, fol. 15v.

9. Stephen Langton, in his marginal commentary on a manuscript of *Historia Scholastica* (fol. 124r) provides a very useful schematization of the ages thus:

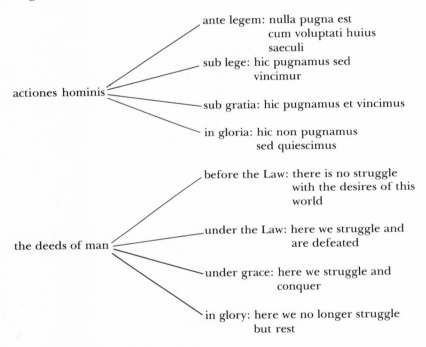

actiones hominis

ante legem: nulla pugna est cum voluptati huius saeculi

sub lege: hic pugnamus sed vincimur

sub gratia: hic pugnamus et vincimus

in gloria: hic non pugnamus sed quiescimus

the deeds of man

before the Law: there is no struggle with the desires of this world

under the Law: here we struggle and are defeated

under grace: here we struggle and conquer

in glory: here we no longer struggle but rest

On this very common notion see further Blenkner 1977:371 and Chenu 1968:182; also see chapter 2 at note 6.

10. "A word's force (*vis*) consists in its meaning"; John of Salisbury, *Metalogicon* 2. 4, trans. McGarry 1962:81.

11. See Patch 1927:81–83 for the conventional association between chess and fortune.

12. Father Blenkner (1977:362, 367–71) argues that Gawain "avoids being foxy" (370). Although I am reluctant to differ from such a fine scholar of the *Gawain*-poet's works, this argument, despite its respect for the manuscript divisions of the poem, seems to me flawed because it does *not* respect Gawain's *lying* like a "thieving merchant."

13. Augustine, *De Civitate Dei* 12. 21 (CCSL 48:379); and see Arendt 1958:177.

Chapter 4

1. For commentaries on and debates about Gawain's terms, see Blenkner 1977:361, 373, 375, 379–80; Burrow 1964:56 (Howard and Zacher 1968: 325–26); Burrow 1965:128–37, 154–59; Farley-Hills 1963:124–31 (Howard and Zacher 1968:311–24); Green 1962:121–39 (Blanch 1966:176–94); Kaske 1979; Silverstein 1977:12–17.

2. See Augustine, *De Libero Arbitrio* 3. 17. 48 (CCSL 29:303–4); *De Genesi ad litteram* 11. 15. 19 (PL 34:436–37); *In Epistolam Joannis ad Parthos* 8. 6 (PL 35:2039)—I owe these references to Kaske 1979; see further the commentary by Gilson 1967:119, 303 n. 12; consult also Gregory, *Moralia in Iob* 14. 53. 65 [*ad* Job 19. 23–24] (PL 75:1074).

3. I base these remarks on the authority of Augustine, *De Civitate Dei* 14. 15 (CCSL 48:436–38) and that of Boethius, *Philosophiae Consolatio* 4. 3 (CCSL 94:70–72).

4. This archetype is faithfully depicted in de Lorris and de Meun, *Le Roman de la Rose* 1974:1, 6–8, 169–235.

5. Johannes Aurifaber, *Determinatio de modis significandi* 3, *ad resp.* 10, 1967: 228.

6. From the gloss *Admirantes* on Alexandre de Villedieu's *Doctrinale* in Thurot 1869(1964):468.

7. Augustine, *Sermo* 107. 7 (PL 38:630); also *De Sermone Domini in Monte Libros Duos* 1. 16. 46 (CCSL 35:52).

8. Wyclif, *Sermons* 1887:1, 90, lines 32–35, quoted in Farley-Hills 1963:127 (Howard and Zacher 1968:315).

9. For helpful bibliography on the pentangle, see (to 1958) Ackerman 1958: 254, n. 1; supplemented by Green 1962:121–39 (Blanch 1966: 176–94); and by Friedman and Osberg 1977:301–3.

10. On the proper or the literal sense, see Augustine, *Contra Mendacium* 10. 24 (CSEL 41:499–502); Quintilian, *Institutio Oratoria* 8. 6. 5, 1978: 5, 105; St. Thomas, ST 1a. 13. 3. For a study of the proper in Patristic denunciations of heretics, with abundant citations, see de Lubac 1961:3, 99–113; consult also Shoaf 1983:34–36; 204–5.

11. For helpful comments on the nature of romance as a genre, see Muscatine 1969:11–13 and Strohm 1971:354–56.

12. On the "crisis" in criticism, see Barthes 1970 and the commentary by Coward and Ellis 1977:25–60; consult also de Man 1971:1–20 and Lentricchia 1980:298–307.

13. As one of those favorably disposed to the argument that Dante influenced the *Gawain*-poet, I find attractive the possible relevance of Bonagiunta da Lucca's *nodo* (*Purg.* 24. 55) to the knots in *SGGK*. (I relegate this discussion to a note because the issue is both extraordinarily complex, in need of further study, and controversial [but cf. Cawley and Anderson 1976:xi–xiii].) In response to Dante's famous declaration of how he composes poetry—"'I' mi son un che, quando / Amor mi spira, noto, e a quel modo / ch' e' ditta dentro vo significando' ('I am one who, when Love

inspires me, takes note, and goes setting it forth after the fashion which he dictates within me')" (*Purg.* 24. 52–54)—Bonagiunta mentions "'il nodo / che 'l Notaro e Guittone e me ritenne / di qua dal dolce stil novo ch'i' odo!' ('the knot which kept the Notary, and Guittone, and me, short of the sweet new style that I hear')" (*Purg.* 24. 55–57). He suggests that this *nodo* is the obstruction that kept his pen from following "'di retro al dittator' ('after him who dictates')" (*Purg.* 24. 61–62). Note—and this is crucial, given Dante's clear willingness to exploit poetically the etymologies of proper names (see especially *Inf.* 13. 59 and 62)—that *Bonagiunta* can be construed to mean "well-joined"; so construed, the name generates considerable irony in the text since he who is "well-joined" constructed "knots" that kept his poetry from being "well-joined" in the "sweet new style."

Be that as it may, the *nodo* is our most pressing concern here. Physically, the appearance of a knot is primarily that of convolution and intricacy. Indeed, 'intricacy' and 'knot' are virtually synonymous, I think all would agree. Thus, if poetry were compared to a knot, the intended sense would obviously be—at least, in the absence of commendation and praise—that such poetry was guilty of arcane obscurity or needless complexity. Something like this, I have no doubt, is Bonagiunta's (and Dante's) meaning. Now, in *SGGK*, not only is the pentangle a 'knot' but the poetry that describes it is also a 'knot', in Bonagiunta's (and Dante's) sense—witness scholarship's extraordinary efforts in recent years to unravel this knot/ poetry (most recently, Blenkner and Kaske have tried their hands at it). The green girdle, on the other hand, is obviously a knot easy to untie— *SGGK* makes so much clear; poetry compared to *this* knot, then, I presume, would be not only not obscure but also, as a consequence, open to the personal (as is Dante's), to the relative and relational, to the tentative—in short, to the human. Such poetry, like the girdle itself, would be open to interpretation (cf. Burrow 1965:158)—rather than closed to all but one *correct* interpretation of its symbols and numerals and figures, and so forth—and that openness would be its human value, its beauty. *SGGK*, we can be thankful, is not a pentangle—it is a poem of a different 'knot'.

I plan a full-length study of the 'knot', in Dante, the *Gawain*-poet, and other medieval poets; crucial to such a study will be St. Augustine's use of *nodum* precisely in the context of interpreting figurative language and figurative actions—see *De Doctrina Christiana* 2. 16. 25 (CCSL 32:50).

14. De Lorris and de Meun, *Le Roman de la Rose*, 1970:3, 148, lines 21543–52, express the medieval understanding of this phenomenon:

> Ainsinc va des contreres choses,
> les unes sunt des autres gloses;
> et qui l'une an veust definit,
> de l'autre li doit souvenir,
> ou ja, par nule antancion,

n'i metra diffinicion;
car qui des .II. n'a connoissance,
ja n'i connoistra differeance,
san quoi ne peut venir en place
diffinicion que l'an face.

Thus things go by contraries; one is the gloss of the other. If one wants to define one of the pair, he must remember the other, or he will never, by any intention, assign a definition to it; for he who has no understanding of the two will never understand the difference between them, and without this difference no definition that one may make can come to anything.

15. On the nearly ubiquitous concept of the *translatio imperii*—brilliantly illustrated in the opening lines of *SGGK*—and its importance to medieval political thought, early and late, see Chenu 1968:138–40 and Curtius 1963:28–29, 384, especially p. 29: "The concept of *translatio*, indeed, implies that the transference of dominion from one empire to another [as from Troy to Britain] is the result of a sinful misuse of that dominion." I, of course, am insisting, in the present case, on both senses of *translatio* so as to emphasize just how Gawain's *sign* works: if only for a brief while, members of the Arthurian court at the end of *SGGK* are incapable of "sinful misuse of dominion" because they have been freed, again if only for a while, by Gawain's sign from *surquidré*—his sign has *translated* them, and therefore the empire need not be translated *from* them.

Bibliography

The Abbreviations list begins on page ix.

Ancient and Medieval Works

Abélard, Peter. *Commentaria in Epistolam Pauli ad Romanos.* Edited by E. M. Buytaert. CCCM 11, 1.

The Advent Lyrics of the Exeter Book. Edited by Jackson J. Campbell. Princeton: Princeton University Press, 1959.

Aegidius Romanus. *Opera Exegetica. Opusculum 1.* "Ad Romanos." 1554/1555. Reprint. Frankfurt: Minerva, 1968.

Amalarius of Metz. *Amalarii Episcopi Opera Liturgica Omnia.* Edited by John M. Hanssens. *Liber Officialis,* vol. 2. Città del Vaticano: Biblioteca Apostolica Vaticana, 1948.

Ambrose, Saint. *De Abraham.* Edited by J.-P. Migne. PL 14:417–500.

———. *De Jacob et Vita Beata.* Edited by J.-P. Migne. PL 14:597–638.

———. *Epistolae.* Edited by J.-P. Migne. PL 16:913–1342.

Angelomus of Luxueil. *Commentarius in Genesin.* Edited by J.-P. Migne. PL 115:107–244.

Aquinas, Thomas, Saint. *Summa Theologiae.* Edited and translated by Blackfriars. London: Eyre and Spottiswoode; New York: McGraw-Hill, various dates.

Augustine, Saint. *Contra Epistulam Parmeniani.* Edited by M. Petschenig. CSEL 51:17–141.

———. *Contra Julianum Pelagianum.* Edited by J.-P. Migne. PL 44:641–874.

———. *Contra Mendacium.* Edited by Joseph Zycha. CSEL 41.

———. *De Civitate Dei.* Edited by B. Dombart and A. Kalb. CCSL 47 and 48.

———. *De Doctrina Christiana.* Edited by Joseph Martin. CCSL 32:1–167.

———. *De Genesi ad litteram Libri Duodecim.* Edited by J.-P. Migne. PL 34:245–486.

———. *De Gratia Christi et de Peccato Originali.* Edited by J.-P. Migne. PL 44:359–410.

———. *De Libero Arbitrio.* Edited by W. M. Green. CCSL 29:204–321.

———. *De Nuptiis et Concupiscentia.* Edited by J.-P. Migne. PL 44:413–74.

———. *De Sermone Domini in Monte Libros Duos.* Edited by Almut Mutzenbecher. CCSL 35.

———. *Enarrationes in Psalmos.* Edited by E. Dekkers and J. Fraipont. CCSL 38–40.

————. *Enchiridion ad Laurentium de Fide et Spe et Caritate*. Edited by E. Evans. CCSL 46:20–114.

————. *In Epistolam Joannis ad Parthos*. Edited by J.-P. Migne. PL 35: 1977– 2062.

————. *In Johannis Evangelium Tractatus CXXIV*. Edited by D. R. Willems. CCSL 36.

————. *Secundam Juliani Responsionem Imperfectum Opus*. Edited by J.-P. Migne. PL 45:1049–1608.

————. *Sermones*. Edited by J.-P. Migne. PL 38, 39, 46, 47.

Aurifaber, Johannes. *Determinatio de modis significandi*. In *Die Entwicklung der Sprachtheorie im Mittelalter*. Transcribed by Jan Pinborg. Beiträge zur Geschichte der Philosophie und Theologie des Mittelalters 42, 2. Münster: Aschendorff, 1967.

Bede. *Homeliarum Evangelii Libri II*. Edited by D. Hurst. CCSL 122.

pseudo-Bede. *In Pentateuchum Commentarii—Genesis*. PL 91:189–286.

Bernard, Saint. *Sermones de Tempore*. Edited by J.-P. Migne. PL 183:35–360.

Bible. Douay - Rheims. 1582, 1609. Thirteenth-century "Paris" edition. Edited by J.-P. Migne. PL 28 and 29.

Biel, Gabriel. *Sermones dominicales de tempore*. Hagenau, 1510.

Boethius. *Philosophiae Consolatio*. Edited by Ludwig Bieler. CCSL 94, 1.

Catholicon Anglicum, an English-Latin Wordbook, dated 1483. EETS 75. London: N. Trübner, 1881.

Chaucer, Geoffrey. *The Works*. Edited by F. N. Robinson. 2d ed. Cambridge, Mass.: Houghton Mifflin, 1957.

Dante Alighieri. *La Commedia secondo l'antica vulgata*. Edited by Giorgio Petrocchi. 4 vols. Società Dantesca Italiana, Edizione Nazionale. Milan: Mondadori, 1966–67. Translated by Charles Singleton. Bolligen Series no. 58. Princeton: Princeton University Press, 1970–75.

de Lorris, Guillaume, and Jean de Meun. *Le Roman de la Rose*. Edited by Felix Lécoy. 3 vols. Paris: Champion, 1966–1974. Translated by Charles Dahlberg. Princeton: Princeton University Press, 1971.

de Meun, Jean. See de Lorris 1966–1974.

Durandus, William. *Rationale Divinorum Officiorum*. Antwerp, 1570.

Gloss *Admirantes* on Alexandre de Villedieu's *Doctrinale*. In MS Bibliothèque de la ville d'Orleans, M252.

Glossa Ordinaria. Venice, 1588.

Gorham, Nicholas. "Distinctiones." MS Oxford Bodl. Hatton 71.

Gregory the Great. *Moralia in Iob*. Edited by J.-P. Migne. PL 75:509–76:781.

The Hereford Breviary. Edited by Walter H. Frere and Langton E. G. Brown. Henry Bradshaw Society 26. London: Harrison & Sons, 1904.

Honorius Augustodunensis. *Sacramentarium*. Edited by J.-P. Migne. PL 172: 737–806.

————. *Speculum Ecclesiae*. Edited by J.-P. Migne. PL 172:807–1108.

Hugh of St. Cher. *Opera Omnia in Universum Vetus et Novus Testamentum*. Lyons: J. A. Hugetan, 1669.

Hugh of St. Victor. *De Sacramentis*. Edited by J.-P. Migne. PL 176:173–618.

John of Salisbury. *Metalogicon*. Edited by Clement C. J. Webb. Oxford: Clarendon Press, 1929. Translated by Daniel D. McGarry. Berkeley: University of California Press, 1962.

Langland, William. *Piers the Plowman*. Edited by W. W. Skeat. 2 vols. Oxford: Oxford University Press, 1886.

Langton, Stephen. Commentary on *Historia Scholastica*. MS Paris B. N. Latin 14414.

Ludolph of Saxony. *Vita Jesu Christi*. Augsburg, 1729.

Migne, J.-P., ed. *Patrologiae Cursus Completus: Series Latina*. Paris, 1844–1864, with later printings.

Mirk, John. *Mirk's Festival* 1. Edited by Theodor Erbe. EETS, ES 96. London: K. Paul, Trench, Trübner, 1905.

Oresme, Nicole. *De Moneta*. Edited and translated by Charles Johnson. London: Thomas Nelson and Sons, 1956.

———. *Le Livre de Yconomique d'Aristote*. Edited and translated by Albert D. Menut. *Transactions of the American Philosophical Society*. New series 47 (5) (1957):783–853.

Pearl. Edited by E. V. Gordon. Oxford: Clarendon Press, 1953.

Pearl, Cleanness, Patience, Sir Gawain and the Green Knight. Edited by A. C. Cawley and J. J. Anderson. London: Dent, 1976.

Cantor, Petrus. "Summa Abel." MS Paris. B. N. Latin 10633.

Petrus Lombard. *In Epistolam ad Romanos*. Edited by J.-P. Migne. PL 191:1297–1534.

———. *Sententiarum Libri Quattor*. Edited by J.-P. Migne. PL 192:519–962.

Prepositinus of Cremona. *Tractatus de Officiis*. Edited by James A. Corbett. Notre Dame: University of Notre Dame Press, 1969.

Quintilian. *Institutio Oratoria*. Edited by Jean Cousin. Paris: Societé d' Edition "Les Belles Lettres," 1975–1980.

Richard of St. Victor. *Sermones*. Edited by J.-P. Migne. PL 177:899–1222.

Rupert of Deutz. *De Sancta Trinitate et Operibus Eius*. In *Genesim*, edited by H. Haacke. CCSM 21.

Sacrum Commercium Beati Francisci cum Domina Paupertate. Edited by Edoardo Alvisi in "Nota al canto XI (versi 43–75) del 'Paradiso' di Dante Alighieri." In *Collezione di "Opuscoli Danteschi" inediti o rari*, 12, edited by G. L. Passerini. Città di Castello: S. Lapi, 1894.

The Sarum Breviary. Edited by Francis Proctor and Christopher Wordsworth. Cambridge: Cambridge University Press, 1879.

Sicard of Cremona. *Mitrale*. Edited by J.-P. Migne. PL 213:13–436.

Sir Gawain and the Green Knight. Edited by E. V. Gordon and J. R. R. Tolkien. 2d ed. by Norman Davis. Oxford: Oxford University Press, 1967. Reprinted with corrections. Oxford: Oxford University Press, Clarendon Press, 1968.

Thurot, Charles. *Extraits de divers manuscrits Latins pour servir à l'histoire des doctrines grammaticales au moyen âge*. Paris, 1869. Reprint. Frankfurt: Minerva, 1964.

Victorinus, Marius. *Commentariorum in Genesin Libri tres*. Edited by J.-P. Migne. PL 61:937–70.

Virgil. *The Aeneid*. Edited by H. Rushton Fairclough. 2 vols. Loeb Classical Library. Cambridge: Harvard University Press, 1974.

Wyclif, John. *Sermons*. Edited by Johann Loserth. Vol. 1. London: Trübner, 1887.

The York Breviary. Edited by Stephen Lawley. Surtees Society 71. Durham: Andrews, 1880.

Modern Works

Ackerman, Robert W. "Gawain's Shield: Penitential Doctrine in *Gawain and the Green Knight*." *Anglia* 76(1958):254–65.

Allen, Judson B. *The Friar as Critic*. Nashville: Vanderbilt University Press, 1971.

Arendt, Hannah. *The Human Condition*. Chicago: University of Chicago Press, 1958.

Barthes, Roland. *S/Z*. Paris: Editions du Seuil, 1970.

Benson, Larry D. *Art and Tradition in "Sir Gawain and the Green Knight."* New Brunswick: Rutgers University Press, 1965.

Bernard, Jacques. "Trade and Finance in the Middle Ages 900–1500." In *The Fontana Economic History of Europe: The Middle Ages*, edited by Carlo M. Cipolla, 274–338. London: Fontana, 1972.

Blanch, Robert J. "The Legal Framework of 'A Twelmonyth and a Day' in *Sir Gawain and the Green Knight*." *Neuphilologische Mitteilungen* 84(1983):347–52.

Blenkner, Louis, O.S.B. "Sin, Psychology, and the Structure of *Sir Gawain and the Green Knight*." *Studies in Philology* 74(1977):354–87.

Boitani, Piero. *Sir Gawain e il Cavaliere Verde*. Milan: Adelphi, 1983.

Bridbury, A. R. *Economic Growth: England in the Late Middle Ages*. London: George Allen and Unwin, 1962.

Burrow, John A. "'Cupiditas' in *Sir Gawain and the Green Knight*." *Review of English Studies* 15(1964):56. Reprinted in Howard and Zacher 1968:325–26.

———. *A Reading of "Sir Gawain and the Green Knight."* London: Routledge and Kegan Paul, 1965.

Cabrol, Ferdinand. "Circoncision (Fête de la)." DACL 3:2:1717–28.

Chenu, Marie-Dominic. *Nature, Man and Society in the Twelfth Century*. Translated by Jerome Taylor and Lester K. Little. Chicago: University of Chicago Press, 1968.

Chydenius, Johann. "The Theory of Medieval Symbolism." Societas Scientiarum Fennica, *Commentationes Humanarum Litterarum*. Vol. 27(2). Helsingfors, 1960.

Courtenay, William J., "Covenant and Causality in Pierre d'Ailly." *Speculum* 46(1971):94–119.

———. "The King and the Leaden Coin: The Economic Background of 'Sine qua non' Causality." *Traditio* 28(1972):185–209.

———. "Token Coinage and the Administration of Poor Relief During the Late Middle Ages." *Journal of Interdisciplinary History* 3(1972–1973):275–95.

Coward, Rosalind, and John Ellis. *Language and Materialism*. London: Routledge and Kegan Paul, 1977.

Curtius, E. R. *European Literature and the Latin Middle Ages.* Translated by Willard R. Trask. New York: Harper, 1963.

Davenport, W. A. *The Art of the Gawain-Poet.* University of London: Athlone Press, 1978.

David, Alfred. "Gawain and Aeneas." *English Studies* 49(1968):402–9.

de Lubac, Henri. *Exégèse médiévale: les quatre sens de l'Ecriture.* 4 vols. Paris: Aubier, 1959–1964.

de Man, Paul. *Blindness and Insight: Essays in the Rhetoric of Contemporary Criticism.* New York: Oxford University Press, 1971.

Derrida, Jacques. *Of Grammatology.* Translated by Gayatri Chakravorty Spivak. Baltimore: Johns Hopkins University Press, 1976.

de Roover, Raymond. *San Bernardino of Siena and Sant'Antonio of Florence: The Two Great Economic Thinkers of the Middle Ages.* Boston: Kress Library of Business and Economics, 1967.

———. *La pensée économique des scolastiques: doctrines et méthodes.* Montréal, Institut d'Etudes Médiévales. Paris: J. Vrin, 1971.

de Saussure, Ferdinand. *Course in General Linguistics.* Edited by Charles Bally and Albert Sechehaye in collaboration with Albert Riedlinger. Translated by Wade Baskin. New York: McGraw-Hill, 1966.

Du Boulay, F. R. H. *An Age of Ambition: English Society in the Late Middle Ages.* London: Nelson, 1970.

Duby, Georges. *The Early Growth of the European Economy: Warriors and Peasants from the Seventh to the Twelfth Century.* Translated by Howard B. Clark. Ithaca: Cornell University Press, 1974.

———. *Rural Economy and Country Life in the Medieval West.* Translated by Cynthia Postan. Columbia: University of South Carolina Press, 1976.

Ellis, John. See Coward.

Englehardt, A. J. "The Predicament of Gawain." *Modern Language Quarterly* 16(1955):218–25.

Farley-Hills, David. "Gawain's Fault in *Sir Gawain and the Green Knight.*" *Review of English Studies* 14(1963):124–31. Reprinted in Howard and Zacher 1968:311–24.

Foucault, Michel. *The Order of Things.* New York: Vintage Books, 1971.

Friedman, Albert B., and Richard H. Osberg. "Gawain's Girdle as Traditional Symbol." *Journal of American Folklore* 90 (1977):301–15.

Gilson, Etienne. *The Christian Philosophy of St. Augustine.* Translated by L. E. M. Lynch. New York: Vintage Books, 1967.

Green, Richard H. "Gawain's Shield and the Quest for Perfection." *English Literary History* 29(1962):121–39. Reprinted in *"Gawain" and "Pearl": Critical Essays.* Edited by Robert J. Blanch. Bloomington: University of Indiana Press, 1966.

Häring, Nikolaus, S.A.C. "Character, Signum und Signaculum." *Scholastik* 30(1955):481–512, 31(1956):41–69 and 181–212.

Hamm, Berndt. *Promissio, Pactum, Ordinatio: Freiheit und Selbstbindung Gottes in der Scholastischen Gnadenlehre.* Beiträge zur historischen Theologie, 54. Tübingen: Mohr, 1977.

Heers, Jacques. *L'Occident aux XIVe et XVe siècles: Aspects économiques et sociaux.* Paris: Presses Universitaires de France, 1973.

Heinzelman, Kurt. *The Economics of the Imagination.* Boston: University of Massachusetts Press, 1980.

Herz, Martin. *Sacrum Commercium: Eine begriffsgeschichtliche Studie zur Theologie der Römischen Liturgiesprache.* Münchener Theologische Studien ser. 2, vol. 15. Munich: K. Zink, 1958.

Hilton, Rodney H., ed. *Peasants, Knights and Heretics.* Cambridge: Cambridge University Press, 1976.

Howard, Donald R. *The Three Temptations: Medieval Man in Search of the World.* Princeton: Princeton University Press, 1966.

————, and Christian Zacher, eds. *Critical Studies of "Sir Gawain and the Green Knight."* Notre Dame: University of Notre Dame Press, 1968.

Javelet, Robert. *Image et ressemblance ou douzième siècle de saint Anselme à Alain de Lille.* Vols. 1 and 2. Paris: Editions Letouzey et Ané, 1967.

Kaske, R. E. *"Sir Gawain and the Green Knight," Proceedings of the Southeastern Institute of Medieval and Renaissance Studies,* 10 (for 1979), edited by G. Mallary Masters.

Kershaw, Ian. "The Great Famine and Agrarian Crisis in England 1315–1322." In *Peasants, Knights and Heretics,* edited by Rodney H. Hilton, 85–132. Cambridge: Cambridge University Press, 1976.

Kottler, Barnet, and Alan M. Markman. *A Concordance to Five Middle English Poems: "Cleanness," "St. Erkenwald," "Sir Gawain and the Green Knight," "Patience," "Pearl."* Pittsburgh: University of Pittsburgh Press, 1966.

Lampe, G. W. H. *The Seal of the Spirit: A Study of the Doctrine of Baptism and Confirmation in the New Testament and the Fathers.* London: Longmans, Green, 1951.

Lentricchia, Frank. *After the New Criticism.* Chicago: University of Chicago Press, 1980.

Levy, Madeleine. See Tigar 1979.

Little, Lester K. *Religious Poverty and the Profit Economy in Medieval Europe.* Ithaca: Cornell University Press, 1978.

Lopez, Robert S. *The Commercial Revolution of the Middle Ages 950–1350.* Cambridge: Cambridge University Press, 1976.

Lottin, Dom Odon. *Psychologie et morale aux XIIe et XIIIe siècles.* 4 vols. in 6. Louvain: Abbaye du Mont Cesar, 1942–1954.

Lyonnet, Stanislaus, S. J., and Leopold Sabourin, S. J. *Sin, Redemption, and Sacrifice: A Biblical and Patristic Study.* Rome: Biblical Institute Press, 1970.

McKisack, May. *The Fourteenth Century: 1307–1399.* Oxford: Oxford University Press, 1959.

Maitland, Frederic. See Pollock 1968.

Malarkey, Stoddard, and J. B. Toelken. "Gawain and the Green Girdle." *Journal of English and Germanic Philology* 63 (1964):14–20. Reprinted in Howard and Zacher 1968:236–44.

Manley, Lawrence. *Convention 1500–1700.* Cambridge, Mass.: Harvard University Press, 1980.

Miskimin, Harry A. *The Economy of Early Renaissance Europe, 1300–1460.* Cambridge: Cambridge University Press, 1969.

Mohrmann, Christine. "Some remarks on the Language of Boethius, *Consolatio Philosophiae.*" In *Latin Script and Letters A.D. 400–900,* edited by John J. O'Meara and Bernd Neumann, 54–61. Leiden: E. J. Brill, 1976.

Murphy, Brian. *A History of the British Economy 1086–1970.* London: Longman, 1973.

Murray, Alexander. *Reason and Society in the Middle Ages.* Oxford: Clarendon Press, 1978.

Muscatine, Charles. *Chaucer and the French Tradition.* Berkeley: University of California Press, 1969.

Oberman, Heiko A. *The Harvest of Medieval Theology: Gabriel Biel and Late Medieval Nominalism.* Grand Rapids, Mich.: W. B. Eerdman's, 1967.

———. *Werden und Wertung der Reformation.* Tübingen: Mohr, 1977.

———. "Fourteenth-Century Religious Thought: A Premature Profile." *Speculum* 53(1978):80–93.

Osberg, Richard H. See Friedman 1977.

Ozment, Steven. *The Age of Reform 1250–1550.* New Haven: Yale University Press, 1980.

Pace, George B. "Gawain and Michaelmas." *Traditio* 25(1969):404–11.

Patch, Howard Rollins. *The Goddess Fortuna in Medieval Literature.* Cambridge, Mass.: Harvard University Press, 1927.

Peck, Russell A. *Kingship and Common Profit in Gower's "Confessio Amantis."* Carbondale: Southern Illinois University Press, 1978.

Pinborg, Jan. *Die Entwicklung der Sprachtheorie im Mittelalter.* Beiträge zur Geschichte der Philosophie und Theologie des Mittelalters 42, 2. Münster in Westf.: Aschendorff, 1967.

Pirenne, Henri. *Economic and Social History of Medieval Europe.* Translated by I. E. Clegg. New York: Harcourt, Brace and World, 1937.

Pollock, Sir Frederick, and Frederic William Maitland. *The History of English Law.* Edited with a new introduction and select bibliography by A. F. C. Milsom. 2 vols. Cambridge: Cambridge University Press, 1968.

Postan, M. M. *The Medieval Economy and Society.* London: Weidenfield and Nicolson, 1972.

———. *Essays on Medieval Agriculture and General Problems of the Medieval Economy.* Cambridge: Cambridge University Press, 1973.

Raw, Barbara. "Piers and the Image of God in Man." In *Piers Plowman: Critical Approaches,* edited by S. S. Hussey. London: Methuen, 1969.

Reichardt, Paul F. "Gawain and the Image of the Wound." *PMLA* 99(1984): 154–61.

Riehle, Wolfgang. *The Middle English Mystics.* Translated by Bernard Standring. London: Routledge and Kegan Paul, 1981.

Rivière, Jean. *Le Dogme de la rédemption chez Saint Augustin.* Paris: J. Gabalda, 1933.

Rörig, Fritz. *The Medieval Town.* Translated by Don Bryant. London: Batsford, 1967.

Ross, James F. "Analogy as a Rule of Meaning for Religious Language." In
  Aquinas: A Collection of Critical Essays, edited by Anthony Kenney. New York:
  Anchor, 1969.
Sabourin, Leopold, S. J. See Lyonnet 1970.
Schnyder, Hans. *Sir Gawain and the Green Knight: An Essay in Interpretation*.
  Cooper Monographs on English and American Language and Literature,
  6. Berne: Francke Verlag, 1961.
Shell, Marc. *The Economy of Literature*. Baltimore: Johns Hopkins University
  Press, 1978.
Shoaf, R. A. "Dante's *colombi* and the Figuralism of Hope in the *Divine Com-
  edy*." *Dante Studies* 93(1975):27–59.
———. "God's 'Malyse': Metaphor and Conversion in *Patience*." *Journal of Me-
  dieval and Renaissance Studies* 11(1981): 261–79.
———. *Dante, Chaucer, and the Currency of the Word: Money, Images, and Refer-
  ence in Late Medieval Poetry*. Norman, Okla.: Pilgrim Books, 1983.
Silverstein, Theodore. "*Sir Gawain*, Dear Brutus, and Britain's Fortunate
  Founding: A Study in Comedy and Convention." *Modern Philology* 62
  (1965):189–206.
———. "The Art of *Sir Gawain and the Green Knight*." *University of Toronto
  Quarterly* 33(1964):258–78. Reprinted in Howard and Zacher 1968:182–
  212.
———. "Sir Gawain in a Dilemma, or Keeping Faith with Marcus Tullius
  Cicero." *Modern Philology* 75(1977):1–17.
Singer, Kurt. "Oikonomia: An Enquiry into Beginnings of Economic Thought
  and Language." *Kyklos* 11(1958): 29–57.
Sohn-Rethel, Alfred. *Intellectual and Manual Labor: A Critique of Epistemology*.
  London: Macmillan, 1978.
Spearing, A. C. *The Gawain-Poet*. Cambridge: Cambridge University Press,
  1970.
———. *Criticism and Medieval Poetry*. 2d ed. London: Edward Arnold, 1972,
  pp. 38–45. Reprinted in Howard and Zacher 1968:174–81.
Spicciani, Amleto. *La mercatura e la formazione del prezzo nella riflessione teologica
  medioevale*. Atta della Accademia Nazionale dei Lincei, ser. 8, vol. 20, fasc. 3.
  Rome, Accademia Nazionale dei Lincei, 1977.
Strohm, Paul. "*Storie, Spelle, Geste, Romaunce, Tragedie*: Generic Distinctions in
  the Middle English Troy Narrative." *Speculum* 46(1971):348–59.
Tamplin, Ronald. "The Saints in *Sir Gawain and the Green Knight*." *Speculum*
  44(1969):403—20.
Taylor, Paul B. "Commerce and Comedy in *Sir Gawain*." *Philological Quarterly*
  50(1971):1–15.
———. "Gawain's Garland of Girdle and Name." *English Studies* 55(1974):
  6–14.
Tigar, Michael, and Madeleine Levy. *Law and the Rise of Capitalism*. New York:
  Monthly Review Press, 1977.
Toelken, J. B. See Malarkey 1964.

Turville-Petre, Thorlac. *The Alliterative Revival*. Cambridge: Cambridge University Press, 1977.

Weiser, Francis X. *Handbook of Christian Feasts and Customs*. New York: Harcourt, 1952.

Williams, Raymond. *Keywords: A Vocabulary of Culture and Society*. New York: Oxford University Press, 1976.

Wilson, Edward. *The Gawain-Poet*. Leiden: E. J. Brill, 1976.

Yunck, John A. *The Lineage of Lady Meed*. Notre Dame: University of Notre Dame Press, 1963.

Zacher, Christian. See Howard 1968.

Index

UNIVERSITY OF FLORIDA MONOGRAPHS
HUMANITIES